THE ARCHAEOLOGY
of the AFTERLIFE

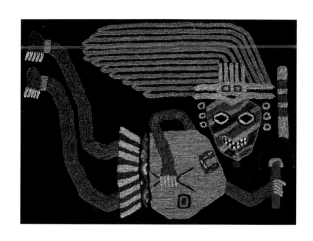

TONY ALLAN

THE ARCHAEOLOGY
of the AFTERLIFE

Deciphering the past from
tombs, graves and mummies

DUNCAN BAIRD PUBLISHERS

LONDON

The Archaeology of the Afterlife
Tony Allan

Conceived, created and designed by
Duncan Baird Publishers Ltd
Sixth Floor
Castle House
75–76 Wells Street
London W1T 3QH

Editor: Joanne Clay
Designer: Gail Jones
Picture Researcher: Susannah Stone
Managing Editor: Christopher Westhorp
Managing Designer: Dan Sturges

British Library Cataloguing-in-Publication Data:
A CIP record for this book is available from the British Library

ISBN: 1-84483-047-0

10 9 8 7 6 5 4 3 2 1

Typeset in Caslon and Syntax
Colour reproduction by Colourscan, Singapore
Printed in Singapore by Imago

A NOTE ON DATES
The abbreviations CE and BCE are used throughout this book:
CE Common Era (the equivalent of AD)
BCE Before the Common Era (the equivalent of BC)

Page 1: An embroidered woollen shroud from Peru's Paracas
culture (ca. 600–100BCE) portrays a warrior with a throwing stick
and a ceremonial knife.

Page 2: Terracotta warriors guard the imperial mausoleum of
China's First Emperor Qin Shihuangdi, who died in 210BCE.

Contents page: Etruscan sarcophaguses from Tarquinia, dating
from the 7th to the 3rd centuries BCE.

CONTENTS

Introduction 6

1 **Africa: Relics of the Old Ones** 8

The First Humans 10
The Egyptian Way of Death 14
The Deir el-Bahri Cache 18
The Enigma of Tomb 55 22
The Tomb of Tutankhamun 26
Glimpses of Past Grandeur 30
The Last Mummies 34

2 **The Americas: Unearthing Lost Worlds** 36

Ancestral Americans 38
The First Mummy-Makers 40
Mummy-Bundles of Peru 44
Cities of the Gods 48
The Lords of Sipán 52
Pacal's Tomb at Palenque 56
Sacrifice at Chichén Itzá 60
Inca Mountain Sacrifices 64

3 **Western Europe: Megaliths
and Mound-Builders** 68

The Earliest Europeans 70
The Alpine Iceman 72
Megalithic Tombs 76
The Mound People 80
Bodies from the Bogs 82

Etruscan Cities of the Dead 86

The Towns that Disappeared 90

Northern Ship Burials 94

The Qilakitsoq Corpses 100

4 **The Near East and Greece:**
From Civilization's Dawn 102

The Jericho Skulls 104

The Death Pits of Ur 106

East of Eden 112

Death in Crete 114

Homer's Heroes 116

The Macedonian Monarch 120

Mountaintop Mausoleum 122

5 **East Asia and the Pacific:**
Emperors and Explorers 124

First Stirrings in Asia 126

The Tarim Basin Mystery 128

The Pazyryk Nomads 132

China's Imperial Tombs 136

Keyhole Tombs of Japan 142

Enigmatic Easter Island 146

Further Reading 150

Index 152

Picture Credits 160

INTRODUCTION

Now that the Earth's surface has been largely explored and mapped, the remaining mysteries mostly lie buried beneath it. Archaeologists are the new Columbuses and Magellans, probing uncharted areas of the past, often on the strength of a hunch, a theory, or a chance discovery.

This book, which takes as its remit the archaeology of death and burial, celebrates some of their most remarkable finds. It pays homage to the landmark investigations that brought to light forgotten realms: the uncovering of Roman Pompeii and Herculaneum, Tutankhamun's tomb in Egypt's Valley of the Kings, Schliemann's historic rediscovery of Troy and the Mycenaean world.

Yet the main focus throughout is on the bizarre and the unexplained – on the past's buried mysteries and on the theories put forward to account for them. Why, for example, were the mummified bodies of seven of the most famous Egyptian pharaohs found bundled into a cliffside tomb in 1881? What persuaded the Inca to take children high up into the Andes and leave them in shallow graves? Who were the enigmatic Caucasoid people whose 3,000-year-old bodies have been recovered, desiccated but relatively intact, from the sands of the Taklamakan Desert on the western borders of China? Why have the corpses of so many victims of extreme violence been recovered from northern Europe's peat bogs?

In seeking to cast light on these puzzles, the book also inevitably touches on the problem of interpretation. Most archaeological finds fit into an established pattern, complementing and perhaps extending a picture of the past already built up from previous discoveries and also from written sources. Many of the examples described in this book, however, broke fresh ground, and in their

below: Stones arranged in circles, ovals, triangles and ship shapes mark more than 600 late-Iron Age and Viking-period graves at Lindholm Hoje in Denmark, Scandinavia's largest burial site.

cases the difficulties involved in making sense of what has been found can become daunting.

To form some idea of the problems involved, imagine for a moment that some intergalactic team of archaeologists touched down on Earth following a nuclear holocaust and set about trying to piece together our own civilization solely from its funerary remains. They might gain an impression of social order from the relative neatness of our cemeteries, and they could gauge something of our state of health from the condition of the bodies. Yet they could have little idea of what we thought, or how we earned our livings, or even the complexities involved in our attitude to death itself. There would also be room for huge misconceptions. What, for instance, might they make of a crematorium, supposing that by some miracle one had survived? Perhaps they would see it as a sacred temple built around a central oven: evidence, some future pundit might suggest, for a form of ritual cannibalism, at which mourners gathered in shaded gardens to dine sacramentally off the dead.

A far-fetched idea, maybe, but useful as a reminder of how easy it is for our own very human archaeologists to misread what they find. The problems are especially marked when dealing with death and its accoutrements because guessing the motives of the actors involved necessarily involves a flight of the imagination. An excavator digging up a building can count on the laws of physics to have some notion of the type of structure its architects set about erecting. Someone trying to work out the meaning of a collection of bones and grave goods, however, inevitably has to enter the mind of the people who laid out the body in that particular way.

Why did the Chinchorro fisherfolk of Peru choose, as much as 7,000 years ago, to disarticulate the corpses of their loved ones and then reassemble them painstakingly with the internal organs removed and bones replaced by sticks? What made the peoples of ancient Scandinavia bury or burn their leaders' bodies in ships? In the absence of reliable literary sources, researchers can only make inspired guesses, drawing on the details of what has been found and also on any other sources of information –

above: Valuable artefacts cover the skeleton of the Lord of Sipán (see pages 52–5), a warrior from the Moche culture which flourished in northern Peru ca. 100–700CE.

historical, geographic, maybe even forensic – that might cast light on those particular societies.

Some patterns, however, re-emerge across cultures in many different parts of the world, and they provide the recurrent themes of the book. The idea of death as a journey, for example, and a need for funerary goods to sustain the deceased in the afterlife were both particularly widespread, at least until a more spiritual understanding of life beyond the grave spread in comparatively recent times. The fact is that death itself remains the final secret, and the varied approaches that people all around the world have taken in the face of its mysteries is what the book is ultimately all about.

THE FIRST HUMANS
THE EGYPTIAN WAY OF DEATH
THE DEIR EL-BAHRI CACHE
THE ENIGMA OF TOMB 55
THE TOMB OF TUTANKHAMUN
GLIMPSES OF PAST GRANDEUR
THE LAST MUMMIES

chapter 1

AFRICA

Relics of the Old Ones

THE FIRST HUMANS

The Sahel region of Chad is a huge, sandy desert where, within living memory, savanna grasses used to grow. Its featureless expanses look like unpromising territory for finding anything of scientific importance, but it was among them, on 19 July 2001, that a student named Ahounta Djimdoumalbaye came across something extraordinary. It was a skull, cracked and deeply weathered, whose most distinctive feature was a massive brow ridge. What made it remarkable was the date assigned to it by Michel Brunet, the French paleontologist in charge of the project: he found the skull to be between 6 and 7 million years old.

The Chad skull – nicknamed "Toumai" – was certainly not that of a man, or of anything much like one. Yet Toumai had a relatively short face, a jaw that protruded less than that of most apes, and relatively small canine teeth – all features that, in Brunet's view, distinguished it from the apes and put it in a direct line of descent to modern humans.

The "missing link"

Toumai is merely the latest in a sequence of dramatic discoveries that have started to fill in the gaps in the human family tree. Ever since Charles Darwin propounded the theory of evolution in the mid-nineteenth century, scientists have sought to prove that humankind and the apes derived from a common stock. Realizing how controversial this view would be, Darwin himself had relatively little to say on the matter. However, brilliant young disciples such as T.H. Huxley had no such qualms, and spelled out in detail the ways in which natural selection could have shaped the unique destiny of the human race. Step-by-step illustrations showing

left: Paleoanthropologist Mary Leakey examines hominid footprints fossilized in volcanic ash at Laetoli, Tanzania. The prints, which are 3.6 million years old, show that hominids were walking upright and on two legs by this date, just like modern humans.

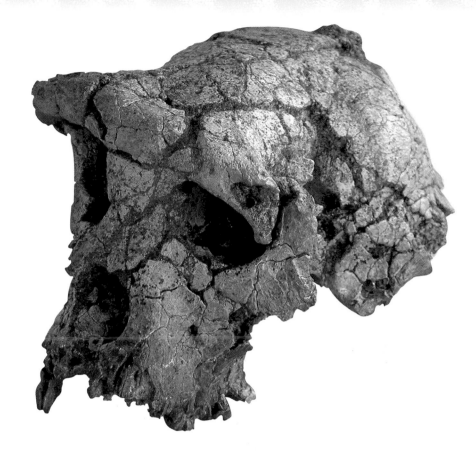

right: Seen from behind, the Chad skull known as "Toumai" – a local word meaning "hope of life" – resembles a chimpanzee's. However, the front view (here) suggests distinct hominid features.

our beetle-browed forebears rising from all fours onto two legs while their sloped foreheads gradually grew domed became familiar classroom tools.

One trouble with Huxley's views was that they remained largely theoretical. At the time when he was writing, there was almost no fossil evidence for the intermediate forms between apes and humans that evolutionary theory required. The hunt began to find the "missing link".

Now, almost 150 years later, great progress has been made in filling in the gaps in the picture, but as much or more work still remains to be done. Increasingly it seems that there were many different branches in the human family tree. As paleontologists seek to piece together early hominids from the remnants of teeth, bones and shattered skull fragments, they are identifying not one but many missing links, some of which coexisted with one another for hundreds of thousands or even millions of years. The search for human ancestry turns out to resemble not so much a straight highway as a dark thicket pierced by many paths, most of which peter out in dead ends. Much more research is needed, and many more fossils will have to be found, before it will be possible to

map with confidence the direct line leading to modern *Homo sapiens.*

The apes to *Homo sapiens sapiens*
Even so, the parameters of the search are at least clearer than they were in Huxley's day. We know that the first step was taken some 30 million years ago, when new kinds of monkey were seen in the rain forests of Africa. The new monkeys dangled on long arms from branches in search of fruit and gradually lost the tail that all earlier monkeys had relied on to retain their balance. These were the apes.

To this day the apes – gorillas, orang-utans, chimpanzees – remain well adapted to life in that lush, tropical world, at least when they are left free of human persecution. But

from about 15 million years ago, climate change began to shrink the forests, forcing some apes to adapt to new conditions. One result was the extinct species *Ramapithecus,* known from fossils dating back 12–14 million years and found as far apart as Spain and China, but particularly in the Himalayan foothills. Only about 4 feet (1.2 m) tall, *Ramapithecus* had lost the daggerlike canines of previous apes and had developed enamel-coated molars, allowing it to move its lower jaw from side to side and grind hard food such as seeds and grain.

If the apes stand at one end of the course of human evolution, the other end is represented by the modern human race, *Homo sapiens sapiens,* and its extinct Neanderthal

cousin, *Homo sapiens neanderthalensis* (also referred to by some experts, who see it as a separate species, as *Homo neanderthalensis*) – now no longer thought of as the epitome of brutishness but rather as an efficient toolmaker who coexisted successfully with *Homo sapiens sapiens* for well over 100,000 years. As *Homo sapiens* first appeared on the world stage only about 160,000 years ago, there remains a gap of more than 10 million years between modern humankind and the early apes. That is the hole in evolutionary history that the fossil hunters have sought to fill.

Homo erectus

Perhaps predictably, the search has mostly led from recent times backward. Evidence for the existence of the immediate predecessor of *Homo sapiens*, *Homo erectus*, was first found not in Africa but in Java by the Dutch paleontologist Eugène Dubois in 1893. The remains of Peking Man, found in the Zhoukoudian caves near Beijing in the 1920s, are also now assigned to this species, and in addition evidence of *Homo*

erectus's presence has now been found in France, Germany, Spain and Algeria, as well as in Africa's Great Rift Valley. The oldest *Homo erectus* finds are at least 1.8 million years old; the species was still thriving a quarter of a million years ago.

Homo erectus – literally, "upright man" – stood as much as 5 feet, 8 inches (1.75 m) tall and weighed maybe 9 stone, 8 lb (70 kg). His brain capacity averaged 950 cubic centimetres: less than today's range of 1,000–1,800 cu cm, but bigger than anything that had gone before. *Homo erectus* apparently lived in small groups, and the fact that the species successfully adapted to the cold climates of Europe and Asia indicates that it had made a vital step forward in mastery over the environment: it had learned to control fire.

Lucy and the Leakey finds

The next, and crucial, step back in human genealogy was dramatically illuminated by two discoveries made by Louis and Mary Leakey at Olduvai Gorge in Tanzania three years apart, in 1959 and 1962. The

second of these had distinctly human characteristics, including the tool-making capacity that won it the scientific name of *Homo habilis* – "handy man". *Habilis* brain sizes were estimated at 500–800 cu cm, just overlapping the lower range of *erectus*'s cranial capacity. The utensils that *habilis* made – flaked-stone hand axes and cutting tools – were used to butcher animal carcasses; some perhaps hunted, but many others scavenged prey species after other, more fearsome predators had brought them down. Even so, the evidence clearly showed that *Homo habilis* had made a crucial transition from a vegetarian to a partly carnivorous diet.

The Leakeys' earlier, 1959 find, had a notably smaller brain, a bony crest like that of a gorilla along the top of its skull, and huge jaws filled with seed-crushing molars that won it the nickname of "Nutcracker man". Although the Leakeys sought at first to place it in a new genus, *Zinjanthropus*, it has since been reassigned as an extreme development of one first discovered 35 years before, this time in South Africa: *Australopithecus*, the "southern ape".

Australopithecus already had a special interest for evolutionists, for its skull was higher and more rounded than those of other apes, and it had teeth that seemed adapted for grinding grain rather than tearing flesh. More remarkable still was the positioning of the foramen magnum –

meant that the creature was almost contemporary with the *Homo habilis* remains subsequently found in the same location. Between 1.8 and 1.7 million years ago, it appeared, both apemen and early humans had coexisted in a single corner of the East African Rift Valley. Suddenly the missing link seemed near.

Since the Olduvai discoveries new finds have cast the spotlight further back into prehistory. One such was made on 30 November 1974, when the American paleontologist Don Johanson discovered most of the

Hunting in Africa

A gap of more than 6 million years still existed between the early apes and Lucy, and that is the one that paleontologists are still struggling to fill. Much of the search has concentrated on the East African Rift Valley. From its Ethiopian end have come two hominids assigned to an even earlier genus, *Ardipithecus*, and dated back between 4 and 6 million years. Another, scientifically labelled *Orrorin tugenensis* but popularly nicknamed "Millennium man" because its discovery in western Kenya was announced in the year 2000, is thought to be more than 6 million years old. The Chad find subsequently pushed the timeframe back toward 7 million years: twice the age of Lucy.

How all these various finds fit together in the larger pattern of evolution still remains to be worked out. The last 20 years have been a time of great discovery, and it may be that a period of consolidation will now follow as fresh finds continue to cast new light on the relationships between the different fossils. For the time being confusion reigns as paleontologists argue over which of the finds represent true advances down the hominid line and which are simply dead ends. Today, the picture of human evolution resembles an uncompleted jigsaw puzzle. The hunt goes on for the missing pieces, and Africa remains the place where they will most likely one day be found.

"It's important to know that we're the sole remaining species. We're one little twig left on the past's complicated tree."

(PALEONTOLOGIST MARY LEAKEY, QUOTED IN *NATIONAL GEOGRAPHIC* MAGAZINE, OCTOBER 2001)

the hole in the base of the skull through which the nerves pass from the brain down the spinal column. In chimpanzees and baboons this aperture lies toward the back of the skull, as their hunched posture requires, but in *Australopithecus* it lay at the bottom of the skull, indicating that the species had walked upright, like humans.

The Leakeys' find was eventually termed *Australopithecus boisei* (although some experts refer to it as *Paranthropus boisei*) and dated to 2.3 to 1.2 million years ago. It was this age that made it extraordinary, for it

skeleton of an early australopithecine in the bank of a dry gully in northern Ethiopia. Christened Lucy, she was barely 3 feet, 4 inches (1 m) tall, even though reckoned to have been a fully-grown adult. The most significant thing about the fossil, however, was its age, which was approximately 3.5 million years. Lucy was eventually assigned a species name of her own, *Australopithecus afarensis*. In 2001 Mary Leakey discovered another genus, *Kenyanthropus platyops*, or "flat-faced Kenya man", which coexisted with Lucy and had a similar-sized skull.

THE EGYPTIAN WAY OF DEATH

No society has left more visible evidence of the ancient dead than Egypt. Even in antiquity, travellers like the Greek historian Herodotus were fascinated by its pyramids, tombs and mummies. In more recent times, interest grew exponentially after the French scholar Jean-François Champollion cracked the mysteries of hieroglyphics in 1824, making it possible for researchers to understand the inscriptions written on papyrus scrolls and tomb walls. In the past decades new techniques ranging from radiology and endoscopy to DNA research have thrown fresh light on the mummies themselves, providing new insights into the mummification process and the health and lifestyles of the individuals concerned.

There was generally nothing morbid about the ancient Egyptians' preoccupation with death. Convinced that the soul survived beyond the grave, they thought it only prudent to make provisions while still in their prime. Foresight was the more important because the realm of death was full of dangers and terrors that only the well-prepared could hope to negotiate. Those who stayed the course, however, could expect to enjoy a satisfactory afterlife that closely resembled the life they had lived on Earth. Tomb imagery often shows the dead eating, drinking, cultivating land and relaxing with their families.

Aspects of the soul

This view of death was complicated by people's multiple conception of the human personality. Egyptians believed that each individual was made up of at least five component parts, over and above the physical body. One element was a person's shadow, another his or her name; to be deprived of either was to risk eternal oblivion. Then there was the *ka*, a sort of spiritual doppelganger that remained in the tomb after death, sustained by food offerings and enjoying the comforts of the funeral furnishings.

In contrast, the fourth element – the *ba* – was mobile; represented in art as a bird with the face of the dead person, it was free to roam at will, whether in the world of the living or among the gods. The final constituent was the *akh*, symbolized as a crested ibis. This was the immortal soul, and it represented the summation of everything that all the other elements sought to achieve.

The first Egyptian mummies

For the *akh* to come into its own, however, a large number of preconditions had to be met. First, the body had to be preserved as completely as possible if it was to be successfully reunited with the *ba* – a necessary step if immortality was to be achieved. It was in this context that the practice of mummification came to prominence during the third millennium BCE. For most of the predynastic period,

"A funeral procession will be made for you on the day of the entombment. The mummy case will be of gold, its head adorned with lapis lazuli. The sky will be above you as you lie upon the bier; oxen will drag you, musicians walking in front of you."

(FROM THE *STORY OF SINUHE*, CA. 2000BCE)

bodies had been laid to rest in shallow graves, where they had been naturally embalmed by the hot, dry conditions. Such circumstances did not apply in the elaborate tombs built first for pharaohs and then, from the Old Kingdom (ca. 2625–2130BCE), for influential courtiers also, and so mummification developed as an artificial alternative.

Mummification practices varied, partly in line with what individuals could afford. By the New Kingdom (ca. 1539–1075BCE), the most sophisticated method involved removing the brain and the internal organs, which were packed in vessels known as canopic jars, in which to be stored in the tomb. The embalmers cleaned out the stomach cavity and filled it with aromatic spices. The corpse was then covered with a naturally occurring salt known as natron, packets of which were also inserted in the abdominal cavity. The body was left to dry out for 40 days, and was then washed and the internal cavity packed with resin and linen. Next came the wrapping of the mummy; various amulets and charms were carefully inserted among the layers of linen bandage to provide magical protection for the dead person in the afterlife. A mask was placed over the face, and then the entire corpse was bandaged once again.

Once the mummy was ready for interment, it was consigned to eternity in some style, accompanied by a procession of servants carrying the tomb furnishings and also by a corps of female mourners, including professionals paid for their services. Before the mummy was placed in its final resting-place, a priest wearing the jackal-headed mask of the god Osiris touched its lips with an *ankh* or life-symbol, thereby magically endowing it with the power to eat, breathe and speak in the next life.

A home for eternity

To ensure that their souls would have access after death to the comforts they had become accustomed to while living, wealthy Egyptians furnished their tombs elaborately and stocked them with magical figurines known as

below: This detail of a wall-painting from the tomb of the 18th-dynasty sculptors Nebamon and Ipuky depicts a ceremony for the purification of the dead: mourners kneel before upright mummies.

*shabti*s that were expected to play the part of servants in the afterlife. The walls were sometimes decorated with vivid wall-paintings showing food and beer or wine; the *ka* was evidently thought to be able to sustain itself from the image of foodstuffs after the actual food offerings left in the tomb at the time of burial, or provided by relatives or priests as part of an ongoing funerary cult, had been used up.

The realm of Osiris

For all the care an individual might take in preparing for death, a terrible ordeal had to be undergone before *ba* and *ka* could be successfully subsumed into the *akh*.

By Middle Kingdom times (ca. 1980–1630BCE), the god Osiris was firmly ensconced as the Lord of the Underworld, a dread realm associated with the west, the direction of the setting sun. When they died, Egyptians expected (at least by New Kingdom days) to go for judgment before Osiris in the Hall of the Two Truths. Reaching the hall involved a long, perilous journey in which the dead person's spirit needed special knowledge to pass the ranks of fearsome guardians that blocked the path. Help was at hand in the form of the Book of the Dead, a prompt-book providing guidance on the correct formulae to employ at each stage of the journey. A copy was generally placed in the dead person's tomb.

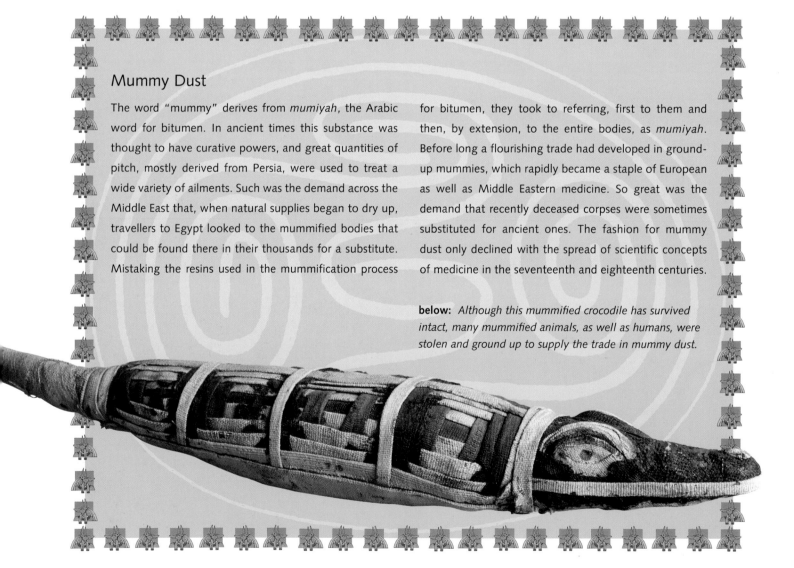

Mummy Dust

The word "mummy" derives from *mumiyah*, the Arabic word for bitumen. In ancient times this substance was thought to have curative powers, and great quantities of pitch, mostly derived from Persia, were used to treat a wide variety of ailments. Such was the demand across the Middle East that, when natural supplies began to dry up, travellers to Egypt looked to the mummified bodies that could be found there in their thousands for a substitute. Mistaking the resins used in the mummification process for bitumen, they took to referring, first to them and then, by extension, to the entire bodies, as *mumiyah*. Before long a flourishing trade had developed in ground-up mummies, which rapidly became a staple of European as well as Middle Eastern medicine. So great was the demand that recently deceased corpses were sometimes substituted for ancient ones. The fashion for mummy dust only declined with the spread of scientific concepts of medicine in the seventeenth and eighteenth centuries.

below: *Although this mummified crocodile has survived intact, many mummified animals, as well as humans, were stolen and ground up to supply the trade in mummy dust.*

If the *ba* successfully overcame all obstacles, it finally found itself before Osiris, who presided over a crucial ceremony known as the Weighing of the Heart. While the *ba* made the so-called Negative Confession, denying that the dead person had done any wrong while living, the heart was balanced on a set of scales against a feather, the symbol of truth. If the scales showed that the *ba* had lied, a fearsome monster known as the Devourer waited to swallow up the evil-doer for ever – a terrible fate referred to as the "second death". If the *ba* was found to have told the truth, however, the deceased could look forward to a happy future in the Fields of Yaru, a well-watered land much like Egypt itself. (In other concepts of the afterlife paradise the deceased became one of the "imperishable stars" or went to join the sun god Re.)

Any brief summary of Egyptian views on death inevitably risks over-simplification; views necessarily varied from region to region in the course of 3,000 years. What did not change, however, was people's awareness of their time on Earth as a passing moment, and an enduring concern for what might come after in their eternal home.

below: The damaged sarcophagus of the pharaoh Ramesses IV (ca.1156–1150BCE) still stands in the main chamber of his elaborately decorated tomb in the Valley of the Kings, western Thebes.

THE DEIR EL-BAHRI CACHE

No rulers have ever taken more care to prepare their eternal resting places than the Egyptian pharaohs, as the huge pyramids that dominate the skyline at Giza still attest. Yet from the earliest times the god-kings were not allowed to rest in peace. Their nemesis was the tomb robber. Whatever elaborate collaboration with corrupt necropolis employees whose job was to protect the tombs.

The problem was so acute by the New Kingdom (ca. 1539–1075BCE), that from the mid-fifteenth century BCE on, the rulers stopped building pyramids, which only served to advertise where their bodies were and craftsmen were policed as closely as modern diamond miners to check that no pilfering took place.

Even so, the thefts continued, and as the order and stability of the New Kingdom's golden age collapsed tomb robbing increased to epidemic proportions.

Around 1120BCE, in the reign of Ramesses IX, an official enquiry was launched, which reported that most of the tombs of nobles and priests in the Valley had been despoiled, although only one pharaonic tomb had by that stage been plundered. The situation worsened after 1070BCE, when Egypt split in two, with the south still ruled from Thebes but the north administered by a rival pharaonic line based at Tanis in the Nile Delta. At some point Thebes' priestly rulers appear to have come to the decision that drastic action was necessary if the bodies of the pharaohs were to be preserved.

"We found the god [Ramesses VI] lying at the rear of the tomb, and the burial place of his queen next to him. We opened their sarcophagi and coffins, and found the noble mummy of the king with a collar upon it and a large number of amulets. A collar of gold was around his neck, and a crown of gold."

(CONFESSION OF A TOMB ROBBER, CA. 1120BCE, TAKEN FROM THE WITNESS STATEMENTS OF THE ENQUIRY INTO TOMB ROBBING ORDERED BY RAMESSES IX)

precautions they took to make their tombs safe – by sealing entrances, building false passages, laying traps, or writing fearsome curses on the walls – intruders still managed to find a way in. Even as far back as the Old Kingdom (ca. 2625–2130BCE), many royal tombs seem to have been pillaged. There is evidence suggesting that the tomb robbers were often the very workmen who had helped construct the pyramids in the first place, sometimes in buried. Instead they chose to be laid to rest in the Valley of the Kings, located in a wild, dry range of mountains across the Nile from Thebes. There their tombs could be hidden in concealed subterranean chambers, while the public rites associated with their death were conducted in mortuary temples built some distance away. The inhabitants of an entire nearby village were employed in digging, decorating and furnishing the tombs; its workers

Neighbours of the pharaohs

The action that the priests took was, of course, secret, and it only came to light almost 3,000 years later – once again through the activities of tomb robbers. Since ancient times the inhabitants of the village of Qurna, in the hills where the Valley of the Kings is situated, had taken a proprietary interest in the treasures it contained. In the medieval era the village was considered a bandits'

nest, and with the dawn of modern Egyptology in the wake of the French emperor Napoleon's invasion of Egypt in 1798 there were open clashes between the villagers and the first European scholars sent to inspect the site. In time, of course, the burgeoning market for Egyptian artefacts worked to the villagers' advantage, as individuals were able to smuggle out objects to sell to dealers in the cities, who then passed them on at much-enhanced prices to European buyers. The takings were slim, however, for the tombs had mostly long since been picked clean.

A secret treasure trove

Sometime early in the 1870s, a village goatherd made a remarkable discovery, not in the Valley of the Kings itself but on the other side of the massif at Deir el-Bahri – the site of the spectacular funerary temple of Queen Hatshepsut. In the hills above the monument, one of the goatherd's kids fell down a hole. On

above: Deir el-Bahri is best known for the mortuary temple of Hatshepsut, visible in the far distance beyond this tomb entrance. The treasure cache lay in the hills behind.

investigation this turned out to be a shaft more than 33 feet (10 m) deep. He went home to inform his family, a well-known local clan called the Abd el-Rassuls. When his kinsmen went to explore, they found they had stumbled upon a previously undiscovered royal tomb, but one quite unlike any other ever uncovered.

"The Screaming Corpse"

One mystery remains from the cache found at Deir el-Bahri. It involves a body found in an unmarked wooden coffin left in the tomb's entrance corridor. Inside it was a whole sheepskin – a material that the Egyptians considered ritually unclean – enclosing the unmummified body of a man who had been bound hand and foot. The dry conditions of the tomb had naturally preserved the corpse. Most strikingly, they had immortalized its contorted face. One observer present when the package was unwrapped in Cairo in 1886 described the ghastly impression the sight made: "I can only say that no countenance has ever more faithfully recreated a picture of such affecting and hideous agony. His features, horribly distorted, surely showed that the wretched man must have been deliberately asphyxiated, most probably by being buried alive." It is thought that this terrible fate must have been the punishment for some unknown crime.

For the better part of the next decade, the Abd el-Rassuls took care to keep their discovery secret. The first that the outside world knew of the tomb's existence was when certain unusually valuable and apparently royal new pieces began to find their way onto the local art market. The Antiquities Service had been set up in Cairo in 1858 to stop the illicit trade in ancient artefacts, and it soon started to show an interest, sending a wealthy American Egyptologist to Luxor to pose as a potential buyer and report on what he could discover. It did not take him long to identify the Abd el-Rassuls as the likely source of the finds.

The Antiquities Service passed on the information to the local authorities, and two of the Abd el-Rassul brothers were arrested. Although they were brutally beaten – one limped for the rest of his life – they refused to divulge their secret. However, soon after they were released another brother agreed to talk; according to some sources, there was a family quarrel over the division of the spoils, but it is equally likely that he simply realized that the game was up. In July 1881 he led Emil Brugsch, the assistant director of the Antiquities Service, to the hidden tomb; for so doing the brother received a substantial cash sum, duly shared with the rest of the family, and was made foreman of the Cairo Museum's Theban excavations. Even so, it was not long before the family was once more in trouble with the authorities over further thefts.

A prestigious mass burial

At the site, Brugsch was lowered down the shaft on a rope. At the bottom he saw an entrance about 3 feet (1 m) high. Squeezing through, he found himself in a sloping corridor clogged with a jumble of mummy cases. Advancing on his hands and knees and peering around by candlelight, he made out here and there the names of high priests and of queens. At the bottom lay a chamber 16 feet (5 m) square. Here his astonishment turned to open-mouthed amazement as he read the names on the coffins: Ahmose, the founder of the New Kingdom; Tuthmose I, II and III, this last probably the greatest war-rior-pharaoh in ancient Egyptian history; Ramesses I; Seti I, another conqueror who expanded Egyptian rule; and, most extraordinarily of all, Seti's son Ramesses II, the Great, whose 67-year reign is often seen as the high point of Egyptian power and glory. Up to that moment, no royal burial had been discovered in Egypt in modern times; now Brugsch had come across the remains of seven of the nation's greatest rulers jumbled together in a single haul.

Unsurprisingly, Brugsch decided he needed to get some air. Worried that his companions' candles might accidentally set the entire treasure trove alight, he stumbled with them back up to the shaft entrance. When he had collected himself enough to explore further, he found a second chamber, this one containing coffins of the family of the 21st-dynasty pharaoh Pinudjem II. It was from this room that the Abd el-Rassuls had taken the objects – including papyrus, small funerary objects and *shabti*s – that they had sold on the Luxor market; the earlier pharaohs had already been robbed of their valuables at some point in antiquity.

Worried that word of the find would attract other tomb robbers, Brugsch made arrangements for the immediate evacuation of the tomb and the transfer of its contents to Cairo. News did indeed spread fast, and when the steamer packed with pharaonic mummies set off for the capital a few days later Egyptian peasants lined the banks for its downstream journey, the women wailing and throwing dust over their heads to mourn the passage of the dead rulers just as they would have done 3,000 years earlier.

Desperate measures

The explanation for the Deir el-Bahri cache seems obvious enough. The Theban rulers of the 21st dynasty – High Priests of Amun, who founded their claim to rule

above: A bust of pink granite portrays Ramesses II, whose mummy was discovered in the Deir el-Bahri cache. The pharaoh is shown wearing the double crown of upper and lower Egypt and holding the crook and flail that were emblems of kingship.

partly on their respect for ancient tradition – removed the mummies of their great predecessors from their tombs, which were no longer safe, and transferred them, after some remedial work, to a more secure resting place in a shaft the priests had prepared for their own burial. The last mummy to be interred there was that of Pinudjem II, who died in the year 970BCE.

The Deir el-Bahri mummies attracted fresh attention in 1976, when the star find, Ramesses II, was flown to France for emergency conservation measures designed to nip incipient signs of deterioration in the bud. Examination of the corpse suggested that the pharaoh, who died aged about 90, probably suffered in his later years from a painfully abscessed jaw and from curvature of the spine, causing him to assume a hunched posture. The scientists also ascertained that Ramesses had auburn hair, which he dyed with henna in his old age. Intriguingly, too, they discovered that his neck had been broken, although the injury almost certainly happened during the mummification process when the corpse was being prepared for burial.

X-rays taken of the mummy of Seti I in the 1970s demonstrated that, unlike his son, he had died young (between the ages of 35 and 40), apparently of natural causes.

THE ENIGMA OF TOMB 55

When English archaeologists Arthur Weigall and Edward Ayrton discovered a previously unknown royal tomb in the Valley of the Kings in January 1907, they unearthed a mystery that is still the cause of much debate among Egyptologists almost a century later. The layout of Tomb 55, as it was labelled, was relatively simple: a stairway led down to a sloping passage that debouched into a single chamber. The burial place, which had been much disturbed in antiquity, dated from the Akhenaten period; protective charms set into the walls bore the name of Egypt's most radical pharaoh.

The religious revolutionary

For much of its 3,000-year lifespan, ancient Egypt was deeply conservative. Yet there was one startling exception: the reign of Akhenaten, the "heretic pharaoh", who ruled ca. 1353–1336BCE at the height of the nation's New Kingdom might. Coming to the throne as Amenhotep IV after the long, peaceful and prosperous reign of his father Amenhotep III, the young pharaoh quickly decided on a change of direction for himself and the country. A religious revolutionary, he determined to replace all the multifarious Egyptian gods with a single divine presence – the *aten*, or sun disc. At a stroke the temples that were a central part of the Egyptian economy and landscape were closed down. Not content with this bombshell, Akhenaten, having changed his own name, also abandoned the nation's capital Thebes, which was closely associated with the priesthood, and built a new one, Akhetaten (now known as Amarna), 250 miles (400 km) to the north.

There he and his beautiful wife Nefertiti, along with their daughters, worshipped the sun in open-air complexes that could hardly have been more different from the dark, multi-columned temples that were the homes of the older gods. To accompany the religious revolution, Akhenaten encouraged a new, naturalistic artistic style, which replaced the stiff, stately grace of traditional Egyptian sculpture.

"As you scatter darkness
As you cast your rays ...
The entire land takes up its work,
All animals content at their business,
Trees and plants spring up,
Birds fly from their nests,
Their wings praising you."
(FROM AKHENATEN'S *HYMN TO THE ATEN*)

The conservative backlash

Akhenaten remains a vastly controversial figure. Some people see him as a great spiritual innovator, pioneering what was in effect the first monotheistic religion; others view him as a ruler who needlessly brought chaos to Egypt on a personal whim. All that can be said with certainty is that Akhenaten did not reign long enough for his radical reforms to put down lasting roots. When he died, apparently of natural causes, within little more than a decade of forcing through his great religious changes, a backlash against his reign quickly set in.

There is some controversy as to what happened to the throne after his passing. A shadowy figure, Smenkare, appeared on the scene shortly before Akhenaten's death. Smenkare may have been Akhenaten's immediate successor, although some scholars believe that Nefertiti first ruled in her own right for a while. However, within a couple of years of Smenkare's own accession, the throne had passed to a much more famous figure, the boy pharaoh Tutankhamun (see pages 26–9), in the course of

right: This limestone stela from a royal tomb at Tell el-Amarna depicts Akhenaten, his wife Nefertiti and two of their daughters offering lotus flowers to the sun god Aten.

The mystery mummy

The most intriguing object in the tomb was a mummy case enclosing a body badly damaged by damp. The mummy case had originally been made for a queen, as the hairstyle of the image on the lid showed, but had subsequently been adapted to house a male occupant; traditionally masculine symbols of royalty, including the uraeus or snake headband and the false beard, had been added. To compound the confusion, the cartouches, or nameplates, had all been blanked out. Seemingly, a coffin prepared for a female royal had at some point been hastily adapted to receive a male occupant.

The confusion extended to the body inside. A doctor who examined the bones at the time of the discovery concluded that they were those of a woman, and the tomb was initially introduced to the world by Theodore Davis, the wealthy American who had paid for the dig, as that of Queen Tiy. However, when they were re-examined in Cairo the remains were declared to have belonged to a man, the view generally held today. Now opinion swung toward the view that the body might be that of Akhenaten, removed by his followers from its original resting-place in Akhetaten at a time when it was becoming apparent that that city was no longer safe. In this view, the heretic pharaoh was buried surreptitiously in the tomb he had originally had cut for his own mother.

However, this interpretation too has run into problems. The body has now been examined by several different medical teams, and the consensus view – although not a unanimous one – is that the remains are those of a youth of between 18 and 25 years of age. Such an age would rule out Akhenaten, who is thought to have been at least in his mid-30s by the time of his death.

As a result, a third name has been put forward for the occupant of the coffin – that of Akhenaten's mysterious successor Smenkare. This theory draws partly on evidence that only became available in 1922 with the opening of

whose short reign Egypt officially abandoned the worship of the *aten* in favour of that of Amun, god of Thebes, and all the other deities of the traditional pantheon. When Tutankhamun died ca. 1322BCE, power passed firmly back into the hands of the old guard in the shape first of a veteran courtier, Ay, followed four years later by an army commander, Horemheb. Under these men all trace of Akhenaten's memory was carefully expunged from Egyptian records; his statues were torn down, his inscriptions defaced, and the city of Akhetaten was demolished.

Tomb 55 appears to date from the end of Akhenaten's reign. Some of the artefacts it contained bore the names – some partly erased – of Kiya, a junior wife of Akhenaten, and of Tutankhamun. The largest objects in the tomb were dismantled panels from a shrine designed to house the sarcophagus of Queen Tiy, Akhenaten's mother. One of these was found inside the entrance, suggesting that an attempt to remove the shrine had been thwarted when the panel got jammed. Yet this was clearly no ordinary tomb robbery. Someone had erased all references to Akhenaten from Tiy's shrine when it was dismantled for removal, evidently at a time when the very name of the heretic pharaoh was being expunged from the historical record.

Tutankhamun's tomb. Medical comparisons made between the body of the boy pharaoh and the occupant of Tomb 55 turned up intriguing similarities. Both shared the same blood group, and the skulls were also morphologically almost identical; undoubtedly the two were close relatives. In addition, grave objects originally intended for Smenkare were found in Tutankhamun's tomb, suggesting that the burial plans for Smenkare had at some point been disturbed.

Unfortunately, Smenkare himself remains a stubbornly elusive figure. He enters history in artwork from Akhetaten only in the last years of Akhenaten's reign, when he is depicted as an intimate associate of the king's, replacing Queen Nefertiti as the monarch's close companion. The evidence is usually taken to mean that Akhenaten appointed him co-regent to help with the burden of government in the last couple of years of his life, and that the younger man later went on to inherit the throne at some point, if only briefly.

Although Smenkare's exact relationship with the pharaoh – whether younger brother or son – remains unproven, one possibility suggests itself. Nefertiti, to judge from the surviving artwork, only had daughters, and in ancient Egypt it was unusual (although not entirely unknown) for women to inherit the throne. It is possible that Smenkare was Akhenaten's son by a junior wife, possibly the lady Kiya.

Smenkare was certainly closely related to Tutankhamun, his successor as pharaoh; they were most probably brothers. We do know that Smenkare's age at death, to judge from the surviving portraits, would have been about 20, fitting in with the available forensic evidence. And however short his reign, he was undoubtedly a king, entitled to the royal regalia depicted on the mummy case. DNA studies on the two mummies might one day further clarify the relationship between the boy king and the unknown cadaver; at the moment the Egyptian government is not allowing the tests. For now, therefore, Smenkare remains the most obvious candidate to be the occupant of Tomb 55. Perhaps this little-known young pharaoh, who lived through such turbulent times, will one day step out of the shadows.

The Search for Nefertiti

In June 2003 a group of scientists led by British Egyptologist Dr Joann Fletcher claimed to have found the long-lost mummy of Nefertiti in a hidden side chamber of Tomb KV35, a royal-mummy cache in the Valley of the Kings. The mummy is one of three that ancient priests left lying on the ground badly wrapped and unnamed, as though disgraced. The other two mummies, of an older woman and a teenage boy, have been tentatively identified as Queen Tiy and Akhenaten's brother; the mummification techniques used suggest the late 18th dynasty. The body that may be Nefertiti's appears to be that of a young royal woman: her shaven head shows the mark left by the tight-fitting brow band worn by royalty; the remnants of a wig in the style favoured by 18th-dynasty royal women was found close by; what appears to be her right arm (broken off by tomb robbers) is bent up at the elbow with clutched fingers, as if it once held a royal sceptre. The mummy also has double-pierced ears, often seen in Nefertiti's portraits. Its mouth has been attacked, perhaps to prevent its spirit from "breathing" in the afterlife.

The identification has caused heated debate among Egyptologists. Sadly, DNA tests will probably not resolve the uncertainty as Nefertiti was not of royal blood and so would not share genetic patterns with other royal mummies.

THE TOMB OF TUTANKHAMUN

The 1922 excavation season was to be make or break for English archaeologist Howard Carter. He and his patron Lord Caernarvon had taken over Theodore Davis' Valley of the Kings concession in 1914, and from 1917 on they had conducted extensive investigations. Yet so far very little had turned up and Caernarvon had made it clear that he would not be funding another season.

Carter's search had been inspired by the work of Davis. Over the years his diggers had turned up various small objects marked with the name of Tutankhamun, the boy pharaoh in whose reign the religious revolution undertaken by the heretic ruler Akhenaten was reversed (see pages 22–5). Carter was convinced the finds represented debris from a pharaonic burial, and that an undiscovered royal tomb lay nearby.

Carter decided to return to an area of ancient workmen's huts that he had cursorily examined at the very beginning of his quest. On the second morning of the dig excited workers reported finding a stone step. For three days Carter worked feverishly to clear the stairway. At the bottom he found a blocked doorway bearing a royal seal. It seemed that he might be on the verge of making a great discovery.

Carter sent a telegram to his patron in England: "At last have made wonderful discovery in valley;

a magnificent tomb with seals intact; recovered same for your arrival; congratulations." On 24 November Caernarvon and his daughter, Lady Evelyn Herbert, arrived at the site and the unsealing began. Yet when the staircase was again cleared, the first signs were not good. Close inspection revealed that the seal on the door had apparently been tampered with at some point in antiquity, not once but twice. Carter immediately feared the worst, although in the event he was to find that, although ancient tomb robbers had indeed penetrated the tomb, they had only removed small items of jewelry.

Opening the tomb

When the threshold was finally breached, it turned out to open onto a corridor filled with rubble. It took several more days of digging to reach a second sealed entrance. This, too,

above: Howard Carter emerges from Tutankhamun's tomb bearing treasures from the first largely undisturbed pharaonic burial to be found in modern times.

bore the insignia of Tutankhamun. At last the moment of truth had come.

Carter made a hole in the upper left-hand corner of the door and passed a lighted candle through it. His eyes took a second or two to adjust to the flickering light. Finally, objects started to come into focus out of the darkness. Impatiently, Caernarvon demanded, "Can you see anything?" Carter replied shakily, "Yes. Wonderful things."

What Carter and his companions saw in the first moments of revelation was in fact only the contents of an antechamber, where grave goods and furnishings were stacked up in a disorderly jumble. Prominent among the confusion were three couches shaped in the form of animals, one lion-headed, another in the form of a cow, a third a cross between a crocodile and a hippopotamus. Such furnishings were familiar from ancient Egyptian artwork, but had never before been seen in real life. Thrown higgledy-piggledy around them were stools, alabaster vases, ebony and ivory gaming boards, and jars of foodstuffs. In another corner were dismantled sections of four royal chariots, their wooden frames sheathed in gold and precious stones.

More treasures were found in a small annex, and the discoveries continued to pile up: a throne backed by a magnificent gilded plaque of the king, in the company of his bride Ankhesenamen, illumined by the sun's rays; no fewer than 35 model boats, many full-rigged; upward of 50 chests containing linen, cosmetics and jewelry.

The burial chamber

Most significantly, Carter found a third sealed door, this one located between two lifesize, gilded wooden statues of the dead king. He quickly realized that Tutankhamun's body must lie in an inner sanctum behind this portal. He forced an entrance into this room also, and found himself in a space filled almost entirely by

right: This elegant head decorated a stopper lid from a compartment in the alabaster chest in which Tutankhamun's internal organs were stored. The figure is thought to represent a protective goddess.

"At such moments the emotions evade verbal expression ... Three thousand years and more had elapsed since men's eyes had gazed into that golden coffin. Time, measured by the brevity of human life, seemed to lose its common perspectives before a spectacle so vividly recalling the solemn religious rites of a vanished civilization. ... Here at last lay all that was left of the youthful Pharaoh, hitherto little more than the shadow of a name."

(HOWARD CARTER DESCRIBING THE MOMENT WHEN TUTANKHAMUN'S MUMMY WAS FINALLY REVEALED)

a gilded shrine, 9 feet (2.7 m) high and more than 10 feet (3 m) long. In a fourth room beyond the royal burial chamber stood a gilded chest, still equipped with carrying poles, topped by a statue of the jackal god Anubis. The deity was seemingly guarding a second shrine, also watched over by statues of goddesses, which turned out to contain the canopic chest holding the king's internal organs, preserved in miniature golden coffins.

The task of removing, restoring and cataloguing the contents of the tomb eventually took nine years. It was complicated above all by the condition of the shrine. This was found to contain three separate, elaborate coffins, stacked one inside the other and all contained within a carved stone sarcophagus. While the two outermost coffins were made of gilded wood, the innermost one was fashioned from solid, 22-carat gold, weighing almost 14 stone (100 kg). Within this central container lay the mummy of the dead pharaoh, the face covered with a magnificent mask of gold inlaid with quartz.

left: A gilded wood statue of the famous boy pharaoh depicted as the god Horus in the guise of a hippopotamus hunter, standing on a papyrus raft while in search of Horus' enemy Seth.

Beneath its many layers of wrapping, which contained 143 protective amulets, the royal skeleton was in very poor condition. Resins applied to preserve it had had the opposite effect, oxidizing it and leaving it black, shrivelled and glued to the inside of the coffin, from which it had to be cut with heated knives.

A fragile king

Examination of Tutankhamun's remains showed the king to have been about 18 years old when he died. An initial autopsy produced evidence of a lesion on the left cheek, while subsequent X-ray examination in 1968 indicated a stray fragment of bone within the skull as well as an area of damage that could have indicated a blow to the head. There is no way of telling whether these injuries occurred before death or after, during the mummification process, but they have contributed to a wave of speculation suggesting that the pharaoh was murdered by rivals eager to seize the throne.

US medics who have recently re-examined the X-rays have found that the king's upper neckbones were fused, perhaps due to a rare condition known as Klippel-Feil syndrome. If he did suffer from this condition, Tutankhamun would have had difficulty turning his neck and would have had to move his whole body to look behind him. The same study found that the young ruler also had a slightly curved spine, meaning that he may have walked with the aid of a stick (a theory seemingly upheld by the 130 walking sticks found with his grave goods). It appears that Tutankhamun was frail, and would have been particularly vulnerable to injury or even death, if he happened to fall over – or was pushed.

Mystery and beauty

For all the wealth of goods in the tomb, there was almost nothing in the way of historical inscriptions to throw further light on the confused political situation that surrounded Tutankhamun's death. One sad personal touch was the discovery of two mummified female foetuses, one dated at about five and the other about seven months. Presumably these were the product of miscarriages that left Tutankhamun and his wife Ankhesenamen childless.

The discovery of Tutankhamun's tomb remains the greatest triumph of modern Egyptology. In all, more than 5,000 objects, many of them startlingly beautiful, were delivered from it to the Cairo Museum. The reign of the boy pharaoh may have been brief, but it took place at a time when Egypt's artistic achievement was at a height. Other eras might have produced grander tombs, but not necessarily ones filled with more "wonderful things".

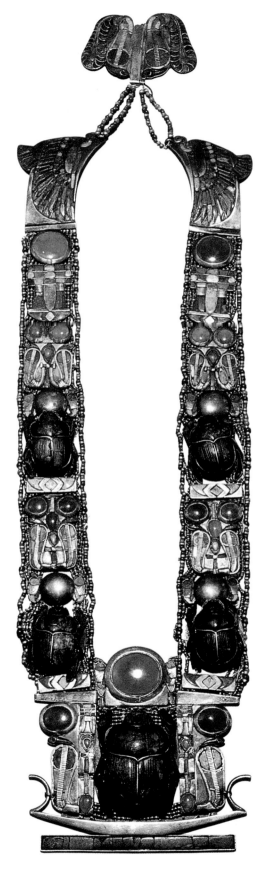

right: The repeated motif of this necklace from Tutankhamun's tomb represents a scarab beetle rolling a ball of dung – the Egyptian symbol for the sun's journey, propelled by the god Re, across the daytime sky.

GLIMPSES OF PAST GRANDEUR

Africa makes up almost a fifth of the Earth's land area, yet for much of its history the bulk of the continent was largely cut off from the rest of the world. Stretching from the Atlantic Ocean to the Red Sea, a band of desert effectively segregated sub-Saharan Africa from Eurasia to the north. The barrier was not impenetrable, and some contacts were maintained, particularly in the east. Yet Africa's isolation, along with the scarcity of written records, has cast a long shadow over its history from which, thanks to archaeology, it is only now starting to emerge.

Nubia

One enduring channel of communication through the desert barrier was the Nile River. Because of the river, the area of sub-Saharan Africa best known to the ancient world was the region that the Romans knew as Nubia, and that the ancient Egyptians knew under a variety of names, the most prominent being Kush. The Kushite realm, centred between the Nile's second and sixth cataracts in what is now northern Sudan, had a long, fraught relationship with Egypt, marked by periods of war but also by much cultural assimilation. For more than a century from ca. 760BCE, a Nubian dynasty ruled Egypt as the nation's 25th dynasty.

Echoes of Nubia's greatness can still be seen in the pyramids marking royal graves at two of the region's historic capitals, Napata – home of the 25th-dynasty pharaohs – and Meroë. Built on a smaller scale than their Egyptian models and with a steeper pitch, the pyramids rise above tomb chambers in which major discoveries have been made. From 1916 on the American archaeologist George A. Reisner excavated the royal cemeteries at El Kurru and Nuri, a few miles from ancient Napata. There he found the tomb of one of the greatest of the 25th-dynasty pharaohs, Taharqa, who ruled from 690–664BCE over an empire that stretched from Nubia to the Mediterranean. Among the grave goods contained in Taharqa's 150-foot (46-m) high pyramid was an array of no fewer than 1,070 *shabti*s – the statuettes that, according to Egyptian tradition, provided domestic service for the dead in the afterlife. Yet Reisner also found evidence for purely Nubian burial customs. One of the most striking was a horse cemetery, which was located within a few hundred feet of the royal tombs at El Kurru. In it royal mounts were buried upright, wearing net shrouds decorated with amulets of pottery, cowrie shell, silver and bronze.

left: The striations on this bronze head pendant, which was unearthed in the course of excavations at Igbo Ukwu in southern Nigeria, are thought to represent ritual scarifications – a sign of social prestige in many African cultures.

Traces of a more sinister Nubian custom were found outside the town of Kerma, the earliest capital of Kush. There Reisner uncovered thousands of graves dating back to the eighteenth and seventeenth centuries BCE. Among them were eight apparently royal tombs, covered by huge, circular, earthen mounds. In the central chambers, the monarchs' corpses reclined on couches of woven rope or palm ribs stretched over wooden frames, while in the corridors around them lay the bodies of literally hundreds of men, women and children, all apparently slain when the dead ruler was laid to rest. In one of the tombs Reisner counted no fewer than 322 separate corpses, the largest number of sacrificial victims ever found in any single burial. That particular Nubian ruler appears to have been buried with his entire household – bodyguards, subordinate wives and their children, and servants.

West African empires

Having flourished for more than 2,000 years, the Nubian kingdoms fell into decline after ca. 350CE. Several centuries were to pass before comparable realms were again to appear in the sub-Saharan lands, this time in West Africa. Islamic influence was strong in the empire of Ghana (located to the north and west of the present-day country of that name), which rose to prominence in the tenth century. Such influences were even more marked in the successor empire of Mali, which grew rich on trade with the North African littoral, conquered for Islam in the eighth century CE, as well as on its own resources, particularly of gold. When the Malian emperor Mansa Musa, a devout Muslim, travelled to Cairo in 1324 on pilgrimage to Mecca, he and his entourage of 15,000 dispensed such quantities of the precious metal that Egypt's currency was destabilized by inflation for several years.

The great West African empires, defended by horsemen wielding lances and bows and arrows, grew

Cemeteries in the Cliffs

Among Africa's most spectacular archaeological sites, the cave tombs of the Tellem people lie in inaccessible crannies high up in the Bandiagara cliffs (see illustration, right), a precipitous escarpment that snakes for almost 125 miles (200 km) across southern Mali. The region is now the homeland of the Dogon, who migrated there sometime in the fifteenth century CE, displacing the earlier inhabitants. According to their legends, the Tellem reached their cliff-face eyries by flying; archaeologists who have explored the caves reckon that they used now-eroded paths. Some of the caves contain the remains of as many as 3,000 people. Among the cult objects associated with the burials are a number of wooden figurines of men with their arms raised in supplication, dating from the eleventh to fourteenth centuries.

up in the savanna country bordering the Sahara's southern flank. Some of their wealth, however, penetrated farther south, into the woodland realms that lay between the savanna and the Atlantic Ocean. This was a region of strong local artistic traditions that, in the case of the Nok sculptures of central Nigeria, stretched back as far as the fifth century BCE. Later manifestations of West African artistic achievement included the naturalistic portraits of rulers produced in Ife (in what is now western Nigeria) from the seventh to the fourteenth century CE, and the celebrated Benin bronzes, produced from the 1400s on.

The Igbo Ukwu bronzes

Evidence of another, previously unknown tradition turned up in dramatic fashion in the village of Igbo Ukwu in southern Nigeria in 1939. A local householder digging a cistern came upon a cache of more than 40 bronze artefacts in a previously unknown style. The castings eventually found their way to the Nigerian Museum, where they attracted the attention of archaeologists and art historians alike.

In 1959, a Cambridge-trained archaeologist, Thurstan Shaw, was dispatched to the village to explore further. He not only found another repository of bronze objects in the original compound, but also came across a ceremonial burial chamber 10 feet (3 m) below the surface of a neighbouring plot. In a wood-lined tomb, a local dignitary had been buried seated on a stool. He wore a copper crown and breastplate and held a fan and a flywhisk. Among his grave goods were a stylized leopard's skull cast in bronze, three ivory tusks, and more than 100,000 glass and carnelian beads. The remains of five other individuals, possibly sacrificial victims, were found above the roof of the tomb.

The most remarkable thing about the Igbo Ukwu find, besides the originality of the bronzework, was the radiocarbon dating associated with it – a date of ca. 850CE was indicated. At the time of Shaw's discovery, many scholars thought it impossible that the sophisticated bronzing techniques and imported materials used could have existed in Africa so early. However, today most experts accept the Igbo Ukwu horde as clear evidence that West Africa's bronze-working tradition is actually several centuries older than had previously been imagined.

Great Zimbabwe

The most famous archaeological site in southern Africa is undoubtedly Great Zimbabwe, whose curving stone walls have symbolized the mystery and romance of Africa's past ever since its remains were brought to the attention of the wider world in 1871 by a German traveller, Karl Mauch. Fancifully, he identified the ruins with the palace of the biblical Queen of Sheba. In fact, Great Zimbabwe comprises the vestiges of a city of the Shona people that was at its zenith of power and wealth in the thirteenth and fourteenth centuries CE. The region had grown rich on gold, copper, iron and tin, even though metal production remained ancillary to cattle herding in the Shona economy. By trading their mineral resources to the coast

"He sits in audience or to hear grievances against officials in a domed pavilion round which stand ten horses covered with gold-embroidered materials. Behind the king stand ten pages holding shields and swords decorated with gold, and on his right are the sons of the vassal kings of his country wearing splendid garments and their hair plaited with gold."

(THE ARAB HISTORIAN AL-BAKRI DESCRIBING AN 11TH-CENTURY CE RULER OF GHANA)

at Sofala 280 miles (450 km) away, the inhabitants of the city were able to build up surplus wealth. The money found its way into the hands of a ruling class that used it to build the masonry enclosures that still inspire wonder to this day.

The prosperity generated by the Great Zimbabwe trading networks extended into the surrounding region, as has been demonstrated by the discovery of fourteenth- and fifteenth-century burials at Ingombe Ilede, 310 miles (500 km) to the northwest on the Zambezi River, in what is now southern Zambia. There the bodies of 46 people were recovered between 1960 and 1962. Most were decorated with jewelry, and they were buried with grave goods that included oddly-shaped copper ingots along with iron hammers, hoes and gongs. Made in an area not previously associated

above: The site at Great Zimbabwe may have been abandoned because of the land's inability to support the royal court's cattle.

with material wealth, the Ingombe Ilede finds suggest that, six or seven centuries ago, southern, like western Africa, had an unexpectedly vital trading economy – one that was largely disrupted by the arrival of European competitors from the sixteenth century on.

THE LAST MUMMIES

Few people know that mummification techniques similar to those of ancient Egypt were being practised on island outposts off the African coast as recently as the fifteenth century CE. The Guanche, indigenous inhabitants of the Canary Islands, were probably the last people in the Old World to perform such rites, continuing to do so until the Spanish conquest of the islands.

Thought to have been descended from the Berber peoples of North Africa, the Guanche were goatherders who showed a predilection for cave-dwelling. At one stage they are known to have had a knowledge of writing because inscriptions using what appears to be an ancient Berber alphabet have been found on the islands, but by the time of contact the art of literacy had been lost.

Information on the religious beliefs of the Guanche is scarce, all evidence of it having been suppressed by the Catholic Church after the Spanish conquest. Those reports that survived suggest the islanders worshipped a supreme being while also recognizing subsidiary deities associated with the moon, the stars and other natural phenomena. Mountains were sacred to them, and they would take libations of goat's milk high into the hills to make offerings. They evidently

below: The volcanic nature of the Canary Islands provided many suitable cave burial sites. Known locally as the Caves of the Guanches, these caverns near Galdar on Gran Canaria are typical of those in which the mummies were laid to rest.

believed in a life after death because they left grave goods with their dead that included food, as well as stone tools, obsidian knives and pottery vessels.

The mummy-makers

Above all the Guanche took care to preserve the dead. Only upper-class individuals were mummified, although some other corpses were naturally preserved by the dryness of the caves in which they were interred. Most of the mummies were destroyed after the conquest, and barely 20 now survive in a good state of preservation, so information about mummification techniques is incomplete. It seems, though, that the viscera were removed, and the corpses were then fleshed out to restore their natural shape with a variety of packing materials, including stones, rolled goatskins and soil. The body was left to dry in the sun for between 14 and 20 days, and was then wrapped in layers of goatskin. The work was done by a professional caste of mummifiers; men worked only on male bodies, women on females. (Some experts believe the Guanche tradition of mummification derived ultimately from Egypt. If so, the link presumably came through the

Berber communities of the North African mainland, who were in cultural contact with Egypt, but the exact mechanisms of transmission remain unclear.)

Once the corpse had been made ready, it was carried to a burial cave, often perched high on a valley side. There the bodies were laid to rest, usually on wooden biers. The cave entrance was sometimes partially blocked with rubble or with dry-stone walling in order to protect the occupants from the elements. On special days mourners would return to the caves to light fires and make offerings.

Following the Spanish conquest the indigenous culture was largely depleted as a result of deportations and enslavement. It is fitting that the mummies on which the Guanche lavished such care have survived among the culture's few remaining memorials.

"The body is perfect in every particular, the bowels are extracted, and the skin appears of a deep tanned copper colour."

(FROM A CONTEMPORARY NEWSPAPER ACCOUNT OF A GUANCHE MUMMY BROUGHT TO ENGLAND IN 1772)

below: Only a few Guanche mummies have survived since the European conquest of the Canary Islands in the 15th century.

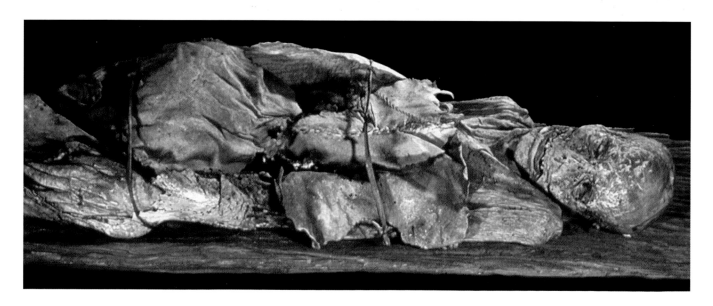

 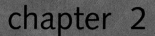

chapter 2

THE AMERICAS

Unearthing Lost Worlds

ANCESTRAL AMERICANS

THE FIRST MUMMY-MAKERS

MUMMY-BUNDLES OF PERU

CITIES OF THE GODS

THE LORDS OF SIPÁN

PACAL'S TOMB AT PALENQUE

SACRIFICE AT CHICHÉN ITZÁ

INCA MOUNTAIN SACRIFICES

ANCESTRAL AMERICANS

People have speculated for centuries about how America was first populated. For a long time there was general agreement about the origins of the earliest settlers; now, however, that consensus is being questioned.

The traditional scenario maintained that the first inhabitants of America made their way from eastern Siberia into the New World across the Bering Straits land bridge, which was exposed during the last Ice Age between 50,000 and 10,000 years ago. Hunters following

game could, it seemed, have made the journey from the Old into the New World without a need for boats.

Challenging the Clovis theory

Until recent decades the scenario went almost unchallenged, and most controversy focused on the date when the crossing was first made. A minority of scientists cited some controversial carbon datings to push the arrival of the first humans back as far as 40,000 years ago, but majority opinion tended to reject those dates as unreliable. As recently as the 1990s, a consensus seemed to be forming that there had been three separate waves of immigration. The first was dated to around 11,500 years ago and involved the people known as "Clovis" because their artefacts were first found at Clovis, New Mexico; they were thought to have pushed south, populating the southern United States and all of South America. The second wave, considered responsible for peopling the northern USA and southern Canada, was thought to have arrived about 10,500 years ago. The third group of incomers consisted of the ancestors of the Inuit and Aleut peoples who settled the far north; their estimated time of arrival was about 10,000 years ago.

This neat picture is today being contested on several fronts. The Clovis immigrants were thought to have moved south down an icefree corridor through Alaska and central Canada. However, recent research suggests that there was no vegetation in the area to support the big game they would have had to hunt on the way; instead, some experts now believe that immigrants might have travelled by boat down the Pacific coast. Then the remains of a village housing about 30 people were found far to the south, at Monte Verde in Chile; the site was unequivocally

left: The wall-paintings – including spray-painted human-hand stencils and numerous depictions of people and animals – that adorn the Cueva de las Manos (Cave of the Hands) in Patagonia, Argentina, are believed to be more than 9,300 years old.

> "We cannot know if he is truly any-one's ancestor. Given the millennia since he lived, he may be sire to none or all of us."
>
> <small>(JAMES C. CHATTERS, THE FORENSIC ANTHROPOLOGIST WHO FIRST STUDIED THE REMAINS OF KENNEWICK MAN)</small>

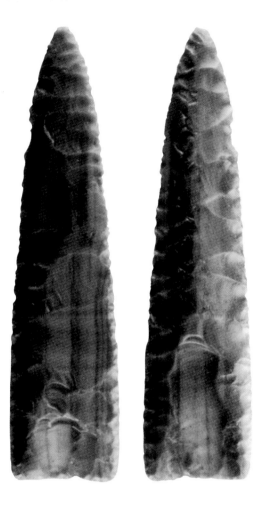

dated back as far as 12,500 years, throwing out the accepted chronology by more than 1,000 years.

Kennewick Man

The most widely publicized challenge to established theories came in 1996, when spectators at a boat race on the Kennewick River in Washington state came upon a skull embedded in the riverbank. Subsequent investigation turned up almost the entire skeleton of a man who stood 5 feet, 6 inches (1.73 m) tall, and who had been 40–45 years old at the time of death. Sometime earlier he had been wounded by a projectile – the tip was found embedded in his right hip – but the wound had apparently healed. When the remains were carbon-dated, they were found to be approximately 9,350 years old.

The most startling thing about Kennewick Man was his facial appearance. He was apparently not Mongoloid – the racial type associated with northeastern Asia and into which all the early American settlers were thought to have belonged. The discovery raised the intriguing possibility that there might have been other waves of immigration not allowed for in the established schema.

Unfortunately, further research on Kennewick Man has so far been prevented as the skeleton has become the object of a prolonged court case. Claiming the bones as those of an ancestor, Native American groups are demanding to have them handed over for repatriation. A group of scientists is requesting the right to continue investigating the find. Kennewick Man remains in a legal limbo until the dispute is settled.

above: These axe heads, which are thought to be more than 11,000 years old, were among the 100-plus objects found in the Anzick cache in Montana in 1968. The cache also contained the skeletal remains of two children, making it the only known Clovis burial site.

Attempts to extract DNA samples from Kennewick Man have so far failed, but it is possible that at some future time improved sampling techniques may produce results. In the light of present knowledge, the most interesting suggestion put forward is that he may represent a physical type not from northeastern Siberia, like the Clovis people, but rather from the central Pacific region. If so, the possibility arises that there were other access points to the New World besides the Bering Straits. The history of American settlement might turn out to be altogether more complicated than had previously been imagined.

THE FIRST MUMMY-MAKERS

Two thousand years before the ancient Egyptians first artificially preserved their dead, mummies were being produced in South America. The culture that made them was not some grandiose empire such as the Inca realm that would one day dominate the entire region west of the Andes. Rather, it was a handful of Stone Age fishing communities in a desert area of the Pacific coast, grouped closely around what is now the Peru-Chile border.

The El Morro bodies

Chinchorro culture takes its name from a beach south of the town of Arica in northern Chile. It was there that in 1917 the German archaeologist Max Uhle came across some unusually preserved corpses.

Although other, similar finds were made in the intervening years, a full realization of just how extraordinary the Chinchorro story was had to wait on a major find made in October 1983, when workers laying pipes for the Arica Water Company came upon traces of an early cemetery on a bluff known as El Morro. In all, 96 bodies were crammed into a space only about 23 feet (7 m) square; 60 of them had been fully mummified. This find, along with other earlier and later discoveries, has permitted researchers to form a remarkably clear picture of how the Chinchorro people lived, as well as of how they preserved their dead.

The Chinchorro survived as fishermen in one of the world's more extreme environments. Much of the Atacama Desert, which borders the Pacific in the Chinchorro region, is totally lifeless. Yet the waters offshore are unusually rich thanks to the Humboldt Current, which sweeps cold, Antarctic water up South America's west coast and attracts huge quantities of plankton that support an abundant marine food chain.

Despite the sea's bounty, however, the area would be uninhabitable without supplies of fresh water for drinking. Then as now, these were provided at fairly regular intervals along the coast by rivers carrying waters from the high Andes less than 60 miles (100 km) away across the desert. The Chinchorro villages lay where these lifegiving streams reached the coast. Each one occupied what was in effect a tiny oasis with its face turned to the ocean, although none was completely cut off either from the mountain hinterland or from its neighbouring communities, similarly located 12–18 miles (20–30 km) away, up and down the coast.

Study of the corpses has shown that the villagers lived on fish, shellfish and seabirds, supplemented by the meat of a few land animals and of sea-lions, which are common on the coast; the only greenery came from wild plants. They made their clothes of animal or bird pelts, or else twined them from wild reeds. Grave goods buried with the mummies included tools, which were mostly made of chipped stone, fish hooks fashioned from bone, cactus spines or mussel shells, net bags for collecting shellfish, and wooden spears.

Roughly a quarter of the El Morro bodies were those of children who had died in their first year, indicating that the Chinchorro endured a high infant-mortality rate; some foetuses were also buried. Even among those who survived infancy, life expectancy was only about 25 years. Roughly 20 percent of the adults bore traces of tapeworm, presumably as a result of eating raw or partly-cooked fish or shellfish. Many of the males also showed signs of an occupational infirmity called auditory exostosis, marked by bony growths in the ear canal – caused by repeated exposure to cold water, it is associated with diving. Almost one woman in five suffered from osteoporosis, now generally a disease of old age; in Chinchorro society it was probably the result of repeated child-bearing, which can cause mineral deficiencies, in combination with a calcium-poor diet.

Self-adornment was clearly important to the Chinchorro; many of the bodies were pierced – the dead were buried wearing earrings and other jewelry – and some were covered with elaborate tattoos. Research has

even shown that the Chinchorro deliberately deformed their children's heads. Pieces of wood or another hard material were tightly bound to infants' skulls for the first year of life to create flat spots.

Chinchorro burial customs

The Chinchorros' lifestyle would have familiarized them with skinning and dissecting, particularly the flaying of sea-lion pelts. It must also have left them with time on their hands, for the waters offshore are so bountiful that a few hours' fishing and shellfish-collecting a day would easily have fed a village.

Some such explanations no doubt lay behind an extraordinary revolution in burial customs that took place in the villages at some point deep in prehistory. The very earliest Chinchorro burials found, which are more than 8,000 years old, simply involved wrapping the dead in furs, reed mats or pelican skins and laying them on their backs in shallow graves, where the dry desert air naturally preserved them. From about 5000BCE on, however, a radical new method was adopted that involved the total transformation of the corpses.

The new technique demanded nothing less than the complete disassembly of the dead body; the individual parts were then stripped of their soft tissue and put together again in a form that was less subject to decay. The first step was to remove the head and limbs, which were either cut off or else perhaps left to decompose until they could be easily pulled away from the rest of the body. The brain was extracted, usually through the foramen magnum (the opening linking the skull to the spinal column), and the torso was cut open to remove the internal organs. Hot coals or ashes were put in the opening to dry out the body cavity. The body was then flayed, except for the hands and feet, which were apparently too tricky to flense and so were left intact. The skin was set aside for later use.

Having stripped the body clean of all its soft parts, the Chinchorro mummy-makers then proceeded to reassemble it. A stuffing of grass, soil, ashes or animal hair, or some combination of all four, was inserted into the brain and stomach cavities, as well as around the limbs to replace the missing flesh. They used fibre twine to tie splints of wood to the spine and to the bones of the limbs in order to support the skeleton. A white ash paste was then spread over the body and skull, where it was worked like plaster to create a flat, mask-like, oval face, complete with stylized eyes, nose and open mouth; it was also moulded to form breasts (on female bodies) or genitals (for males). The skin of the face was then replaced, and the scalp, complete with hair, was glued back on; pieces of sea-lion skin were sometimes employed for patching. Finally, the mummifiers used brushes made from dried grass and a paste of manganese and sand to paint the head and body black.

"As we arrived, the scene was mesmerizing: a profile of the trench revealed several of the mummies lying on their backs, lined up in a row, as if they were travelling together through eternity when their trip was unexpectedly interrupted. The mummies' black, shiny faces glistened against the brown, sandy soil of the bluff."

(Anthropologist Bernardo Arriaza, describing his first sight of the El Morro mummies in 1983)

Unique mummy-makers

In the absence of any written or oral records, one can only hypothesize why the Chinchorro took such care to reconfigure their dead. The fact that the earliest mummies were all of children and foetuses has led some experts to suggest that mummification began as an attempt by grief-stricken parents to keep their dead children with them. Later, all members of society were mummified; the Chinchorro community, it seems, was remarkably egalitarian, even in death. Some bodies were evidently repainted on more than one occasion, suggesting that the mummies were kept for display for some time before being buried. The wooden splints that served to keep the limbs rigid make it likely that the bodies were propped up, either in standing or sitting positions. Whether they were kept permanently on view around the village or were only disinterred for special occasions is not known.

The production of the mummies seems to have continued uninterrupted for more than 3,000 years – longer than ancient Egypt's entire dynastic history. The only significant change in procedures came ca. 2500BCE,

after which date the bodies were painted red rather than black. At the same time, the process of mummification became rather less elaborate: the limbs were no longer disarticulated, but simply had incisions cut into them to allow the flesh to be removed and wooden splints inserted. Other bodies were smoked over fires, to dry them out, and then coated with a cement of mud and sand as they lay in the grave.

The Chinchorro mummy-makers were unique. They came up with their techniques entirely unaided, several millennia before any other culture pursued the idea of mummification. Once the practice had started, it continued for an extraordinary length of time, only being abandoned ca. 2000BCE (after which desiccated bodies were simply covered in a layer of mud and buried). Most startlingly of all, the methods used involved a far more radical butchering of the corpse than those employed by any other mummy-making culture.

right: The painted parts of Chinchorro mummies such as this black example found at El Morro were buffed up with a pebble or a smooth piece of wood to give them a smooth, glossy finish.

MUMMY-BUNDLES OF PERU

When the Spaniards conquered the Inca empire in the sixteenth century CE, one of the features of the vanquished civilization that most astonished them was the treatment accorded to its dead rulers. Following a monarch's demise, his internal organs were removed and were buried with much pomp; some of the deceased's wives and servants went to the grave with their defunct lord.

The rest of the ruler's body, however, was not interred. Instead, it was preserved in unrevealed ways, and was then wrapped in layers of fine cotton. The bound mummy was dressed in gorgeous royal raiments and returned to the palace where the king had lived before his death. There it was put in the care of his *panaca*, a lineage group that was made up of the ruler's descendants in the male line. These faithful attendants took

care to see that the dead monarch continued to be treated with all the respect shown to him when he was alive. Offerings of food and drink were regularly set before the mummy, and servants were on hand to whisk away flies; one even lifted the corpse from time to time, purportedly to allow it to urinate.

The dead ruler's activities were not confined to the palace, for he was also expected to play a continuing role in public life. In the words of one bemused Spanish chronicler, officials " ... brought the royal mummies, lavishly escorted, to all the most important ceremonies, sitting them down in the plaza in a row, in order of seniority. ... It was also customary for the dead rulers to visit one another, and they held great dances and revels". From time to time the mummies were taken to the

left: A mummy-bundle from Paracas, wrapped in a mantle. The textile designs and the type and range of enclosed goods enabled the living to express a great deal about the personality of the deceased.

"The bodies were so intact that they lacked neither hair, eyebrows nor eyelashes. They were in clothes just as they had worn when alive, with bands on their heads but no other signs of royalty. They were seated in the way Indian men and women usually sit [cross-legged], and their eyes were cast down ... . The bodies weighed so little that any Indian could carry them from house to house in his arms or on his shoulders."

(CHRONICLER GARCILASO DE LA VEGA DESCRIBING INCA ROYAL MUMMIES IN 1559, SHORTLY BEFORE THEIR DESTRUCTION BY THE SPANISH AUTHORITIES)

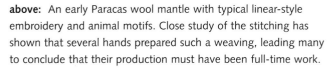

above: An early Paracas wool mantle with typical linear-style embroidery and animal motifs. Close study of the stitching has shown that several hands prepared such a weaving, leading many to conclude that their production must have been full-time work.

palace of the reigning monarch, who would seek their advice, relayed through the chief officers of the *panaca*s.

A spectacular discovery at Puruchuco-Huaquerones, the site of a shantytown on the outskirts of Lima, has recently revealed that it was not only the Inca rulers whose remains were preserved after death. The bodies of more than 2,200 people, rich and poor, young and old, have been found buried there, many in the form of mummy-bundles. Some, presumably members of the Inca élite, still wore the headdress feathers that were a sign of their high status in life.

The Inca empire came at the very end of ancient Peru's long history, enduring for less than a century before its conquest by Spanish *conquistador*s in the

1530s. Yet the custom of preserving the bodies of revered ancestors was an old one, dating back more than 2,000 years, that it had inherited from earlier cultures.

The hidden tombs of the Paracas peninsula
A spectacular discovery made in 1925 highlighted just how enduring the tradition of preserving the dead was. For some time previously, remarkable Peruvian textiles had been turning up on the international art market, raising suspicions that tomb-robbers had made a major find. The source was finally traced to the Paracas peninsula, a desolate region of the Pacific coast about 155 miles (250 km) south of the present-day capital, Lima, and 370 miles (600 km) north of the old Chinchorro homeland (see pages 40–42).

The barren, lifeless peninsula seemed an unlikely place to find anything of value. However, around a hill of multicoloured sandstone called the Cerro Colorado, there were signs of regularly spaced indentations that the last Chinchorro mummies. Much had happened in Peru in the intervening centuries, which had seen the transition from hunting and gathering to a more settled, agricultural way of life. These changes had left their mark on the way that the coastal peoples treated their dead.

To begin with, there were more grave goods than in Chinchorro times, and these now included golden ornaments as well as foodstuffs and ceramics. There were other signs of social stratification too, replacing the easy egalitarianism of the Chinchorro fishing villages. The so-called "cavern" tombs around the Cerro Colorado were occupied not by bodies of all ages and sexes, but for the most part by elderly males, presumably clan elders. And in place of the equal treatment accorded to all the Chinchorro bodies, some of the Paracas mummies were adorned very magnificently indeed.

Bodies in bundles

At Paracas, as at many other Peruvian sites, the main way of demonstrating a mummy's status was through textiles. Typically the body was buried in a seated posture, with the legs flexed tightly up against the chest, set on a mat of cotton or deerskin within a large basketwork structure. Tunics and ponchos were wrapped around the torso, and additional parcels of clothing were stuffed around it; the head was bound in a turban. The completed mummy-bundle could weigh as much as 20 stone (150 kg).

Covering the whole, pyramid-shaped bale were splendid ceremonial mantles, elaborately embroidered in many colours and with intricate designs. Some of the bundles contained more than one mantle; one held 18, along with 46 other garments and 10 gold pieces.

There has been much controversy over the years as to whether the Paracas bodies were mummified naturally or

turned out on investigation to be the entrances to tombs. Some were as much as 16 feet (5 m) deep, approached down sloping tunnels. These were found to house group burials, containing up to 60 separate corpses.

Over the next three years a Peruvian archaeologist, Julio Tello, investigated these burials as well as others, for the peninsula was found to shelter several different cemeteries, in some of which the bodies were buried in individual, rather than communal, graves. The earliest dated back to ca. 500BCE, more than 1,500 years after

The Woman of Ancón

Of the many thousands of mummy-bundles that have been found across Peru, relatively few have reached scientific investigators undisturbed. One that did was found near the town of Ancón in 1976. The body inside was that of an unidentified woman of modest means who had died sometime in the Inca period about 600 years ago. The body, dressed in a sleeveless tunic, had been placed on a sheet with its legs crossed. A wicker workbasket containing weaving equipment lay on the woman's chest, and cloth parcels of food, rings and a rare spondylus shell surrounded the corpse. The head rested on a cotton pillow scattered with coca leaves. A large, beige shroud had been wrapped around the body and then sewn up tight.

Three further layers of wrapping surrounded this first package, and in each one there were further offerings of leaves, foodstuffs and artefacts, including more weaving materials. Wooden poles had been inserted between the third and fourth layers to provide supports for the pall-bearers to hold, and the outermost covering was enmeshed in rope netting. The entire funerary package weighed 155 lb (70 kg).

artificially. Tello himself took the latter view. Subsequent investigators, however, have found no sign of interference with the corpses, and have inclined to the opinion that they were simply left to dry out naturally in the desert air. Some scholars believe that the sitting position in which the mummies were preserved may have helped the process by enabling the action of gravity to drain away internal fluids.

Oddly, many of the individuals buried at Paracas had been deliberately deformed while still alive. There had evidently been a fashion at the time for elongated heads, for the skulls of most of the corpses showed signs of having been bound or clamped within wooden boards in childhood. Even more bizarrely, many also showed signs of trepanation: holes had been cut in their skulls with stone knives and fragments of bone removed. Because many of the wounds showed signs of healing, it appears that even these procedures had been performed while the individuals were alive. It is not known whether the operation was carried out for medical or magical purposes.

The custom of burying the dead in mummy-bundles may already have been ancient even when the Paracas necropolis was created, to judge from four bodies dated back to between 2000 and 4000BCE that were found in the Tres Ventanas cave in the Chilca valley of central Peru. The mummy-bundle tradition continued across much of Peru up to Inca times, although different regions and cultures had their own customs. In several areas, for example, the bundles were adorned with false heads, which were often painted in bizarrely stylized ways.

The people of the Ica valley, inland from Paracas, created long-haired mummies with elaborately braided coiffures. The mummies of the Chiribaya region of southern Peru often had tattoos of animals or abstract designs on their fingers, hands, arms, legs or backs. A cache of mummies of the Chachapoya people has been found high in the Andes; they were distinguished by the embroidered decorations on the plain outer layer of the bundles, including simplified, circular faces above the spot where the real one would have been.

Only the arrival of the Spaniards and the forcible imposition of Christianity finally put a stop to the tradition of mummy-bundles; from the time of the conquest, only Christian forms of burial were tolerated.

CITIES OF THE GODS

In Mesoamerica in the second century CE there was a city as big as early imperial Rome, embellished with monuments rivalling the pyramids of Egypt in size. Yet no one now knows the real name of the lost metropolis, or the identity of the people who built it. Over the past century, archaeologists have sought to unlock its secrets, and among the discoveries they have recently made are mass burials of more than 100 individuals thought to have been offered up as sacrificial victims.

below: Teotihuacán's Avenue of the Dead, as seen from the top of the Pyramid of the Moon. To the left stands the Pyramid of the Sun, beneath which a natural lava cave has been discovered. Caves were sacred to the Mesoamericans and it is thought that the cavern may have been a pilgrimage site even before the pyramid was built over it.

> "All the earth is a grave and nothing escapes it. Nothing is so perfect that it does not descend to its tomb. Rivers, streams and water flow, but never return to their joyful beginnings; anxiously they hasten to the vast realms of the rain god."
>
> (The Aztec ruler Nezalhuacoyotl, musing on the futility of human endeavour)

Today, the city is known by the name the Aztecs gave to its remains in the thirteenth century CE, more than 500 years after its destruction. Overwhelmed by the size and splendour of the ruins, they called it Teotihuacán, the City of the Gods, and made it the scene of one of their most cherished creation myths. They would eventually build their own capital less than 30 miles (50 km) away. Yet Teotihuacán had risen to greatness more than a millennium before the first Aztecs arrived. By the fourth century BCE, it covered a ground area of about 8 square miles (20 square km) and had a population of maybe 150,000 people.

One of the many mysteries surrounding Teotihuacán is the ethnic identity of its citizens. Before the city's appearance, the Valley of Mexico where it lies had been something of a backwater. Located almost 5,000 feet (1,500 m) above sea level, the region had, however, many natural advantages. The climate was temperate, there was abundant rain-fall, and the soil was well-suited to maize and other crops. By the first century CE the richness of the valley's farmland was providing the food surpluses necessary for urban development, and the city began to grow.

Another local factor helped its development, for it lay close to one of central America's largest deposits of obsidian – the hard volcanic glass used to make sharp blades at a time when the continent had no iron. Teotihuacán's workshops turned out obsidian implements that were traded all over Mesoamerica.

Sacred monuments

Whoever they were – and the available evidence suggests that they were simply the local peasantry turned citizens – the first Teotihuacános planned their city on a grand scale. Mesoamericans already had a tradition of ceremonial centres that had first been established by the Olmecs of southern Mexico almost a thousand years before. Whoever designed the layout of Teotihuacán followed their example by planning two separate monuments, which were completed by 200CE. They are now known by the names the Spanish gave them: the Pyramid of the Sun and the Pyramid of the Moon. Both were vast, and they were connected by an equally imposing thoroughfare, the Avenue of the Dead.

The Pyramid of the Sun is the larger of the two. It is stepped, rising from a 740-foot (225-m) square base to a height of about 200 feet (63 m)

right: A ceramic seated figure with an idol in its chest niche, which was found in Teotihuacán. Such statuettes were sometimes buried with sacrificial victims.

and incorporating 1 million cubic metres of sun-dried brick and rubble.

Teotihuacán's third great monument is the Citadel, which stands where the city's main east–west thoroughfare crosses the Avenue of the Dead. This complex incorporates an 11-acre (4.5-hectare) plaza that was presumably a meeting place for the citizens, as well as another stepped building decorated with carved images of the Feathered Serpent – the symbol of the enduring central American deity that the Aztecs knew as Quetzalcoatl.

Buildings of death

When archaeologists investigated the Temple of Quetzalcoatl in the 1980s they came upon a mass burial pit near its southern edge containing 18 bodies. The position in which the skeletons were found, with arms tucked behind their backs and wrists crossed, indicated that they had been sacrificed. Further investigation revealed an identical cache on the north side of the pyramid. All the bodies were facing outward; accoutrements and weaponry buried with them suggested that they were soldiers whose function was to guard the building even in death.

When the excavators moved toward the centre of the pyramid, they found further mass graves. The central one contained 20 male skeletons, presumed to have been people of high rank from the grave goods buried with them, which included almost 600 greenstone artefacts and

more than 800 obsidian objects. Among the odder findings was a skeleton wearing a collar adorned with nine human upper jaws, complete with teeth. A staff topped with an image of the feathered serpent suggested that some at least of the dead may have served as priests.

It came as no surprise to find burials associated with the building's foundation; as early as 1906, the remains of children had been unearthed under the Pyramid of the Sun, where sacrificial victims were apparently buried at each of the four corners of every tier. Recently human remains have also been discovered within the Pyramid of the Moon. These included 17 human

skulls, possibly decapitated, and four male sacrificial victims. The young men had been buried beside the skeletons of dogs, cats and birds of prey, all of them symbols of military orders, suggesting a highly regimented, hierarchical society. Another grave contained the remains of a single individual surrounded by precious objects. Two pumas, several birds of prey and three serpents were interred with him; all appear to have been buried alive.

However, the investigating team were taken aback by the sheer number of bodies that the Temple of Quetzalcoatl concealed; well over 100 have been identified so far, and researchers think that the final total

The Tombs of Tlatilco

In 1936, brickworkers digging for clay stumbled upon clusters of early graves in Tlatilco, now a suburb of Mexico City. The remains they found proved to be unexpectedly early, dating back as far as 1200BCE, to a time when the Olmecs were first introducing monumental art and the building of cities to central America.

At that time Tlatilco was no more than a provincial village, whose inhabitants buried their dead in layered graves beneath their homes. Even so, the quality of the goods interred with them was surprisingly high. Mostly these took the form of terracotta vessels and figurines, often shaped in witty and inventive ways. A few may have come via trade routes from the Olmec lands, but most were locally made, attesting to a level of artistic achievement previously unsuspected at that date in the region.

may be close to 200. Who the individuals were, and how many of them went involuntarily to the grave, are questions that remain unanswered. Mexico's first great metropolis came to a fiery end in the seventh century CE when ravagers – maybe foreign invaders, or perhaps its own rebellious citizenry – tore down the grand staircase of the Pyramid of the Moon, uprooted the platforms and columns of its palaces, and put the city to the torch. With it went most of its secrets, for it left no written inscriptions to answer questions about its past.

The legacy of Teotihuacán

Some of Teotihuacán's traditions survived in distorted form, to resurface among the successor civilizations that replaced it in the Valley of Mexico. The first to rise from the power vacuum following Teotihuacán's destruction was the Toltec state, which in time produced a lost city of its own, Tollan. This capital, which flourished ca. 900–1200CE, was mythologized by the Toltecs' Aztec successors as a tropical paradise, adorned with palaces fronted with gold and turquoise, and inhabited by brilliant artists and craftsmen. When the remains of the city were finally identified by Mexican archaeologists in the 1930s, it came as a disappointment to find that its surviving sculptures were crudely executed and showed an alarming obsession with death and sacrifice, including the provision of skull racks for the heads of decapitated

above: This terracotta mask painted in ochre and cream dates from 350–650CE, the height of the Teotihuacán culture.

enemies and of supine *chacmool*s – reclining figures bearing dishes on their stomachs that served as receptacles for sacrificial human hearts.

All of these traditions would in turn be inherited by the Aztecs, who also fell heir to the Teotihuacán custom of burying the remains of sacrificial victims in the foundations of buildings. In 1980, excavators working on the Great Temple in the Aztec capital of Tenochtitlán came across the remains of 42 children aged between three and seven at the time of death; they had apparently been offered up to the rain god Tlaloc, one of the temple's two patron deities.

THE LORDS OF SIPÁN

Late one night in February 1987 Walter Alva, director of the Brüning Archaeological Museum in the north Peruvian town of Lambayeque, was summoned to the local police station. This was not unusual, for grave-robbers were active in the area and archaeological goods often changed hands on the black market. But Alva was unprepared for the wealth of goods awaiting his inspection. The 33 artefacts

much of it a region of desert striated by river valleys. The genius of their civilization lay in the creation of massive irrigation schemes that put precious water to optimal use. Populations soared as the supplies of crops such as maize increased.

Alva learned that the finds had come from a site located by tomb robbers some days earlier; the thieves had fallen out over the spoils, and one of them had tipped

below: The body of the Moche warrior-priest dubbed the Lord of Sipán was found surrounded by precious ornaments, including a gold face-mask covering the lower part of the skull from cheek to chin. Seashells from Ecuador surrounded the legs and feet.

"For long seconds breath and words would not come; only a ripple of birdsong drifted into the excavation to break the enchanted silence. When we finally spoke, it was to babble: 'A coffin! It's sealed. ... Never opened!'"

(WALTER ALVA, THE EXCAVATOR OF THE SIPÁN TOMB, AS REPORTED IN *NATIONAL GEOGRAPHIC* MAGAZINE)

the police had recovered included a tiny golden head with lapis lazuli eyes, peanuts moulded in gold at three times their natural size, and curious, fang-toothed faces of gilded copper. All were products of the Moche culture that had flourished in northern Peru ca. 100–700CE.

The Moche culture may have survived for 600 years, but it was never a huge empire. At their peak, the Moche only controlled some 500 miles (800 km) of coastal Peru,

off the police. They had uncovered the objects in raids on the looters' homes, in the course of which one local person had been shot dead.

The discovery turned out to have been made in the ruins of an adobe platform adjoining a pyramid mound on the edge of the valley. Excavating there was not easy; armed police guards had to be posted around the clock to scare off treasure hunters.

At first Alva and his team concentrated on the tomb that the robbers had already looted, in search of anything that they might have missed. However, the real thrill of discovery came when they turned their attention elsewhere, noticing a spot on the platform where the adobe blocks had been replaced by soil. Thinking that the loose earth might conceal another burial, they started digging.

Tomb of the Moche lord

Alva and his team soon came on the remains of a wooden chamber about 3 feet (1 m) deep. In it they found a rich cache of the pottery for which the Moche have long been famous. Soon after, they made more sinister discoveries. First, they found a man's skeleton in the foetal position; then, further down, the body of another man about 20 years old, buried with a shield and helmet that showed him to have been a warrior. Grotesquely,

his feet were missing. Alva came to see the young soldier as an entombed guardian, probably sacrificed to protect his master in death as in life; he wondered if the feet might have been deliberately amputated to indicate symbolically that he would never leave his post.

The question of who the sentry might have been guarding was answered soon after, when Alva penetrated what Peruvian archaeologists had long dreamed of: the undisturbed tomb of a Moche lord. The lord himself was buried in three blanket shrouds inside a wooden coffin. Around the body were grave goods ranging from a bundle of javelins to magnificent headdress ornaments fashioned from gold and copper. Everywhere there were symbols of status: feather ornaments, pectorals, banners decorated with copper figures, gold bells and rattles, and expensive, imported spondylus shells.

There were also other bodies surrounding the primary burial. Flanking the main coffin were two more bearing the bodies of men, both about 40 years of age. One was interred with a copper shield and war club, indicating that he had been a warrior. The other, perhaps an attendant, had been laid to rest with his head opposite his master's feet; by the attendant's legs, and so directly facing the lord's head, was the skeleton of a dog, maybe a favourite pet.

Two other coffins lay at the head and feet of the principal one. Each of these contained the remains of a woman aged about 20. Initially Alva assumed that these were wives or concubines who had been sacrificed at the time of the lord's death. Further analysis of the skeletons, however, indicated that the bodies must already have been partially decomposed when they were placed in the tomb, suggesting that the women had died at some earlier time. Their corpses may have been interred, or simply stored in a dry place, only to be reburied with the lord when he was finally laid to rest.

All around the coffins caches of pottery were arranged in serried ranks. Further research beneath the coffins revealed the bones of two sacrificed llamas, while in a corner of the tomb excavators came across the body of a young child, seated with his back against an angle of the chamber. He had died at around the age of nine.

Who was the lord who had been buried in such an elaborate fashion? The Moche had no writing, so there

left: Discovered at the Sipán burial site, this intricate Moche ear decoration depicts a warrior. Similar pieces also found at the site showed a deer and a Muscovy duck – both animals known to have been hunted by Peruvian nobles.

Moche Warrior-Priests

The Moches' settled agricultural life encouraged the development of elaborate ceremonial centres – complexes of stepped pyramids and platforms that developed in almost all the major valleys. And the religion to which the temples were dedicated was a bloodthirsty one, whose deities demanded payment in human lives in return for the blessings that they conferred.

Partly to satisfy the gods' requirements, the Moche fought wars in which brightly-clad warriors confronted each other with maces and copper-headed axes. The losers were led with ropes around their necks to places of sacrifice – or were carried on litters if they were aristo-crats, for class distinctions survived even in the face of death. To communicate with the gods and to lead their warriors in battle, such a people needed chiefs who com-bined the status of high priests and military commanders. The lords of Sipán were such leaders; the opulence of their burials attests to the prestige attached to their office.

were no tablets or inscriptions to aid in his identification. However, the Moche did leave a testament to their civilization in their pottery and other artworks, and close study of the iconography of their decorations has allowed researchers to recon-struct much about their world.

One ceramic bottle has proved especially relevant to the Sipán bur-ial. The fine-line drawing encircling it depicts a sacrificial ceremony. Captive prisoners of war are shown having their throats cut and a goblet presumed to contain their blood is presented to a central warrior-priest figure. Similar scenes are in fact known from other Moche artworks, but in this particular example there is an extraordinary similarity between the accoutrements worn by the priest and those found in the tomb, including the crescent-shaped

headdress, rattle and ornamental backplate. In the illustration, as in the tomb, the central figure is accompanied by a small dog.

The correspondences between the burial and the pottery decoration are, in fact, so exact that one leading researcher has suggested that the individual laid to rest at Sipán may be the very man shown in the line drawing. Not knowing the exact title that such a personage might have borne in Moche society, Alva styled him the Lord of Sipán.

The Old Lord

Two years later Alva made another, even more spectacular find at the same site. Upon further investigation it became apparent that the Moche had added layers to the platform structure for more than 200 years; six levels have now been identified.

The Lord of Sipán was buried in the uppermost, most recent level, labelled Level 7. On Level 1, the earliest level, Alva and his team discovered another undisturbed burial – one that was even richer than the first. The tomb contained the remains of a young woman and a middle-aged male thought to have been a warrior-priest – perhaps an ancestor of the powerful lord buried in Level 7. Alva called this new man, whose burial dated from ca. 100CE, the Old Lord of Sipán. Judging from his grave goods, the Old Lord must have been at least as important as his namesake. The many gold, silver and copper ornaments found in his tomb included a solid-gold backflap and a spectacular gold necklace composed of 10 large beads, each depicting a spider with a body bearing an image of a human head.

PACAL'S TOMB AT PALENQUE

Of all the civilizations of ancient America, that of the Maya is in some ways the most surprising. Most of the early cultures grew up in river valleys where agricultural productivity was high, providing plentiful food surpluses to feed the cities. Yet the Mayans flourished in the rainforest terrain of southern Mexico and Guatemala, which even today is notoriously unsuitable for farming. Somehow, by careful husbandry and swamp reclamation, a host of city-states survived and prospered. From the late centuries BCE up to about 900CE, the Mayans built magnificent ceremonial centres and produced some of the world's most elegant artworks. Then, equally mysteriously, they lost their long battle against the jungle, and the trees closed around the sites again.

The rediscovery of Palenque

For hundreds of years afterward, the abandoned cities lay forgotten. They were first rediscovered in the late eighteenth century CE, when a new wave of historical curiosity stimulated a taste for ruins. In 1773 reports of "stone houses" at a place called Palenque (then in the Spanish province of Guatemala but now in the Mexican state of Chiapas) attracted the attention of an antiquary named Ramon Ordoñez, who sent a small expedition to the site. Reports of his discoveries eventually attracted the attention of the Spanish king, Charles III, and subsequently of his son Charles IV. Further expeditions were arranged, and by the end of the century the name of Palenque was firmly established in scholarly circles as a site of historical and archaeological significance.

Even so, Palenque remained remote and difficult to reach, and it continued to guard many of its secrets. It was not until 1949 that the Mexican archaeologist Alberto Ruz Lhuillier set about examining its monuments in detail for traces of earlier structures beneath them. In particular he was attracted by the Temple of the Inscriptions, a stepped pyramid with a stone temple on its summit. The structure took its name from a band

"It was a moment of indescribable emotion for me when I slipped behind the stone and found myself in an enormous crypt which seemed to have been cut out of the rock – or rather, out of the ice, thanks to the curtain of stalactites and the chalcite veiling deposited on the walls by the infiltration of rain-water during the centuries. This increased the marvellous quality of the spectacle and gave it a fairy-tale aspect."

(ARCHAEOLOGIST ALBERTO RUZ, DESCRIBING THE MOMENT WHEN HE FIRST ENTERED PACAL'S TOMB)

of glyphs on the temple's inner rear wall that at that time had not yet been deciphered.

The pyramid's secrets

Ruz noticed that one of the stone slabs forming the temple floor had a double row of holes around its edge, stoppered with stone plugs. Intrigued, he wondered if there might be something concealed beneath. He soon found that others before him – probably treasure-seekers – had tried to raise the lid, only to be discouraged by what they found under it: a mass of rubble and large stones. Ruz, however, pressed on. Before long he came across the capstone of a stepped arch, then a stone step, and finally a staircase that led down through the centre of the pyramid. It was blocked throughout its length by a filling of boulders and clay and it was to take Ruz 10 months' labour, spread over a three-year period, to clear it. In all,

the staircase descended in 67 steep steps to a depth of some 72 feet (22 m) – the height of the temple floor above ground level. There it debouched onto a corridor blocked with a solid mass of stone mortared with lime.

When Ruz's workmen had cleared this obstacle, they found themselves facing a triangular slab of rock about 6 feet, 6 inches (2 m) high. In front of the stone they discovered a rudimentary tomb containing the jumbled skeletons of six young people. Ruz guessed that these might be sacrificial victims, buried at the threshold of some mighty lord's resting place.

above: The Temple of the Inscriptions in Palenque crowns the only pyramid in Mesoamerica built from its inception as a burial chamber. Upon completion the temple, and probably the pyramid too, would have been painted a deep, dark red, typical of all the city's buildings.

The moment of truth came on 15 July 1952 when the workmen displaced the slab just enough for Ruz to squeeze through the opening it concealed. He found himself in a vaulted chamber lying about 5 feet (1.5 m) below ground level. Stucco images of nine life-size figures lined the walls. A stone monument almost filled the

below: The lid of Pacal's sarcophagus, the central panel of which portrays the ruler at the moment of his death. The king is shown wearing a turtle necklace that represents his rebirth as the mighty maize god, with whom he often compared himself.

crypt, topped by an elaborately carved slab. On investigation, this proved to be the tomb that Ruz had expected.

A burial fit for a king

Raising the lid of the tomb was a major task, for the stone slab topping it weighed 5 metric tons and measured more than 86 square feet (8 square m). It was also extraordinarily precious, as the carving incised on its outer surface was one of the finest Mayan artworks ever found (see illustration, left).

When Ruz's team eventually managed to lift the slab they saw that it concealed a cavity sealed by a tight-fitting stone cover. The space beneath was found to contain the skeleton of a single man, rather bigger than average size. A life-sized mask of jade had been placed over his face, but at some point had slipped sideways, eventually disintegrating into hundreds of fragments. Jade glinted elsewhere against the vermilion-coloured walls of the tomb, for the dead man had gone to the grave richly adorned; he wore a diadem, ear plugs, necklace, pectoral, bracelets and rings, all made of the precious green stone. Outside the sarcophagus were further valuables, including pottery vessels, a jade collar and mask, and two fine stucco heads that may have been portraits of the dead man.

It was obvious, from the prestige of the site and the sumptuousness of the burial, that Ruz's find was one of great archaeological significance. Even so, its full stature was not realized for another 20 years, when epigraphers made breakthrough advances in the understanding of Mayan script that allowed the inscriptions on the temple to be deciphered. It then became apparent that the occupant of the tomb was none other than Pacal ("Shield"), one of the greatest and longest-lived of Palenque's rulers. Born in

603CE, he had come to the throne at the age of 12 in 615 and ruled the city-state until his death on 31 August 683. The temple itself was dedicated in the year 692, in the reign of Pacal's son Chan-Bahlum ("Snake-Jaguar"); its construction had evidently been started while Pacal was still alive, but only completed nine years after his death.

Pacal's journey to Xibalba

Close study of the carved sarcophagus lid revealed interesting information on Mayan attitudes to death. The carving shows Pacal descending into the jaws of Xibalba ("Place of Fright"), the underworld to which all who met peaceful deaths were destined to descend, for, according to Mayan beliefs, only those who died violently could expect to ascend to the celestial realm. He is portrayed sitting in a bowl of the type used to offer up sacrifices to the gods, while behind him rises a symbolic, cross-shaped representation of the world tree that linked the various layers of the Mayan cosmos: underworld, Earth and heavens. A fantastic bird, also known from other world-tree images, rests on top of the tree, while around it are symbols of the planets, moon and sun.

As for Pacal's likely fate in Xibalba, that can be deduced from other Mayan sources. Rather like their ancient Egyptian counterparts (see pages 14-17), those who penetrated Xibalba's depths had to face many dangers; but unlike Egyptian souls, the Mayan dead had to rely not on learned formulae, but rather on their wits to survive the wiles of the underworld's malevolent guardians. Only those who successfully negotiated Xibalba's nine separate layers could hope to escape the guardians' clutches and rise triumphantly to the sky as heavenly bodies. Many researchers believe that the nine

left: Archaeologists have painstakingly restored Pacal's jade mosaic funerary mask. The eyes are made of shell and obsidian.

steps of the pyramid under which Pacal was laid to rest represent those layers – and, by extension, the ordeal that awaited the king once his body had been laid to rest.

The Red Queen

In 1994 archaeologists at Palenque discovered another remarkable burial, deep inside Temple 13, which stands next to the Temple of the Inscriptions. Unlike its larger neighbour, Temple 13 had not been built over a tomb – instead, a vaulted burial chamber had been carved out of the already extant pyramid structure. Inside lay a sarcophagus covered with a large limestone slab and containing the remains of a woman aged 40–45. Her body and the numerous jade and pearl objects, bone needles and shells that surrounded her were all covered in red cinnabar, earning her the nickname of "the Red Queen". On her head was a diadem of flat, round jade beads and, like Pacal, she had once worn a green death mask – hers appears to have been made of pieces of malachite. Such rich grave goods – the only tomb in the city more lavish than this one is that of Pacal himself – suggest that this was a woman of very high status. The tomb contains no inscriptions to identify her, although archaeologists have tentatively dated the burial to ca. 600–700CE, the century dominated by Pacal's long rule. DNA testing on the remains of both the Red Queen and Pacal is currently underway and may eventually reveal whether the two were related. Meanwhile we can only wonder who this important woman could have been, and what role she might have played in the life of one of the greatest Mayan kings.

SACRIFICE AT CHICHÉN ITZÁ

Dissatisfied with his wife, Chaac, the rain god, was angry; so upset, in fact, that he inflicted a drought on Mexico's northern Yucatán region. It was his way of registering displeasure and requesting a more attractive bride. In response, the priests of Chichén Itzá selected a beautiful young girl; she was feted and prepared for a new, married life ahead – and the centrepiece of the wedding was an act of human sacrifice.

For centuries local people repeated tales of this sort about Chichén Itzá, but in spite of the existence of a few surviving Mayan texts and some partisan records made by Spaniards such as the notorious destroyer of Mayan written sources, Friar Diego de Landa, it was not possible to gauge with any accuracy what had actually taken place. In the twentieth century CE, however, enough material evidence began to emerge for scholars to compile a reasonable picture of the religious practices of the region.

The Sacred Cenote

Chichén Itzá was one of the Yucatán peninsula's last great cities; its scale and magnificence suggest that it must have been a site of vast religious and social significance. Its main temple complex and its ballcourt were the work of the Itzá people, who built and governed the city from the late tenth to the late twelfth century CE. There is firm evidence from the buildings of strong Toltec influences at work (see pages 62–3) – not least the association of the site with the god Kukulcán, a form of Quetzalcoatl. The Itzá themselves, though, may well have been Mayan.

below: The view from Chichén Itzá's Temple of the Warriors, with its reclining *chacmool* figure (right), toward the pyramid of El Castillo, also known as the Temple of Kukulcán. The pyramid's nine terraces symbolize the nine underground worlds of the cosmos, and it is thought that priests performed human sacrifices there.

The name Chichén Itzá means "Opening of the Wells of the Itzá", in reference to two limestone sinkholes, or *cenote*s, that provided fresh water in a largely riverless region. The larger of the two is known as the Sacred Cenote, so called because of the belief that the life-giving rain deity was present there. The temples and pyramid of the principal site were, and still are, linked by a ceremonial pathway, or *sacbé*, to the Sacred Cenote. Revered by the Maya people of Yucatán, the *cenote* was known to the Spanish as the Well of Sacrifice.

In 1904 American explorer and archaeologist Edward H. Thompson decided to try to establish whether human sacrifices really had been made at the Sacred Cenote. Having purchased the place for $500, he prepared himself for the task ahead by taking lessons in deep-sea diving. Next he bought a mechanical dredge, equipped with winch, tackles and a swinging boom, in the hope that, by dredging up items from the well's depths, he could discover whether the stories were rooted in fact.

Between 1904 and 1911, Thompson recovered some 30,000 artefacts from the *cenote*. The pieces included

" . . . to carry out these sacrifices, they would purchase the children of slaves, or else those of people who out of devotion delivered [up] their children, who were greatly regaled until the day of the feast."

(DIEGO DE LANDA, SPANISH FRIAR AND CHRONICLER, WRITING IN 1566)

bells made out of gold and copper; engraved jade, gold and copper plaques; and intricately worked gold and jade discs. The material he discovered spans eight centuries and provides a valuable insight into both cult practices and the political, economic, social and religious change within Mayan civilization. One curious fact that Thompson noted was that many of the objects had been broken before being thrown into the well – it is thought

left: Dating from the 9th to 13th centuries CE, this Mayan jade pendant was recovered from the Sacred Cenote. It depicts three figures with lances, but the meaning is unknown.

and sacrifice, from the city's vast ballcourt (see box, opposite) to the *tzompantli* or "wall of skulls". Here as elsewhere in Mesoamerica, defeated warriors were often singled out for death, and yet almost none of the skeletons found in the well's depths were those of young males of military age. Such individuals probably met their fate at the top of the steeply inclined pyramid known as El Castillo ("the Castle"; see illustration, page 60); there their hearts were cut out with obsidian knives and their bodies were then hurled down the steps to form a jumbled heap at the bottom.

Such savage rites were not typical of the Mayan city-states, but they were common in the Toltec state that dominated the Valley of Mexico, 745 miles (1,200 km) to the west, in the ninth and tenth centuries CE. The close architectural parallels between Chichén Itzá and the Toltec capital of Tollan (see page 51) have attracted much attention over the past decades, and have sparked huge controversy. For a time it was largely accepted that Chichén Itzá had risen to prominence in the Mayan Classical period, ca. 600–800CE, but had then fallen on hard times. According to this interpretation, the Itzá people then made an alliance with peoples from the Valley of Mexico that revivified the city at a time when most Mayan centres were in terminal decline. The influence of the immigrants explained the Toltec cast of the city's buildings of the post-Classical period, which largely replaced the earlier structures, as well as the penchant for human sacrifice that also manifested from about 925CE on.

This account of the city's history has recently been challenged, as radiocarbon datings taken at various sites have not confirmed the clear break that it suggests; some of the buildings assigned to Toltec times now

that this was done to simulate a ritual "killing" gesture, as though the objects were live sacrifices.

Thompson also found human remains that lent credence to the idea that sacrifice was practised at the well. In all, he found parts of 50 skeletons – a smaller number than might have been expected from the chronicles, although others might have worked their way down into the layer of mud 40–50 feet (12–15 m) deep at the bottom of the pool, or else have been carried off by the underground river that feeds it. The remains were mostly those of children, although elderly men and women were also represented. There was little evidence to support the belief, popular in Spanish times, that the preferred sacrificial victims were young maidens.

Toltec influence?
The Sacred Cenote was not the only place in Chichén Itzá where victims were offered to the gods. The whole complex is in fact full of reminders of blood

seem to date from earlier eras when a northern influence is harder to explain. Even so, the Toltec presence is hard to gainsay and, curiously, there is a compelling legend from the Valley of Mexico that serves to bolster it.

The story, which survived in Aztec versions long after the Toltec realm had disappeared, told of a fabled Toltec ruler named Topiltzin. In his reign the worship of the fierce war god Tezcatlipoca was set aside in favour of a new cult devoted to the benevolent Quetzalcoatl, the famous feathered-serpent god. Topiltzin himself was so closely associated with the cult that he even took the god's name.

As the Aztecs told the story, Topiltzin-Quetzalcoatl presided over a golden age of plenty in which artistic and cultural achievement reached a pinnacle. But the devotees of Tezcatlipoca were biding their time, and

eventually they struck back. According to one version of the legend, the god himself descended to Earth to drive Topiltzin from Tollan. All accounts agree that Topiltzin-Quetzalcoatl was driven from the Toltec capital. One version of the tale maintains that he left with a few devoted followers on a raft made of serpents, sailing eastward across the Gulf of Mexico. This story dovetails neatly with Yucatán legends, recorded in Spanish colonial days, that tell of the arrival in the peninsula of an individual named Kukulcán – the local term for Quetzalcoatl – who was said to have gone to Chichén Itzá. Taken together, the myths would appear to suggest a lingering folk-memory of Toltec emigrants arriving among the Itzá. If so, the incomers evidently brought with them not the benevolent cult the Aztecs spoke of, but something altogether more bloodthirsty.

The Macabre Skull Motif

Among the many reminders of the grisly events that probably took place at Chichén Itzá, some of the most powerful imagery is provided by depictions of human skulls – a death motif that is almost universal. Columns and walls throughout the city are decorated by skull masks (see illustration, right), which symbolize death, warriors and sacrificial victims. Death imagery is prominent at Chichén Itzá's ballcourt, the largest in Mesoamerica, where the balls that decorate the walls bear skulls at their centre. By analyzing the site's bas-relief sculptures, scholars have built up a picture of a literally deadly ballgame, at the end of which the captain of the victorious side decapitated the captain of the vanquished one. A sculpture on a wall panel records just such a victory ceremony, carried out using an obsidian blade. Chichén Itzá's macabre association with skulls also extends to the Sacred Cenote. A skull of a boy, painted

blue with a pink nose and gums, that had been used as an incense burner, was dredged from the waterhole by Edward H. Thompson in the early twentieth century.

INCA MOUNTAIN SACRIFICES

On 8 September 1995 the American mountaineer and anthropologist Johan Reinhard and his Peruvian climbing partner Miguel Zárate were approaching the summit of Mount Ampato, a snow-capped 20,700-foot (6,300-m) peak in the Andes of southern Peru. Its neighbour, Sabancaya, was spewing a plume of lava and ash high into the sky, and Reinhard had wanted to take a close look at an active volcano. One effect of the eruption, however, had been to coat Ampato's upper reaches with a blanket of warm cinders, and the heat had melted the summit ridge. Rocks and stones had fallen away down the slope; some, it would turn out, had once formed part of a ceremonial platform, built many centuries ago almost on the mountain's summit.

The Ice Maiden's resting place

Amid the ash and ice, Zárate was the first to spot a dash of colour. He and Reinhard both quickly recognized the reddish feathers of the headdress of an Inca ceremonial statuette. They knew what such a sign meant – the site must have been used for rituals performed in honour of mountain gods at the time of the Inca ascendancy 500 years previously.

The two men guessed that other objects from the ceremonial site might have rolled down from the summit, along with sections of the platform. Sure enough, further down the slope they discovered what they were looking for: an Inca burial bundle. With infinite care they carried their precious burden, its weight swollen to 80 lbs (36 kg) or more by its encrustation of ice, down the mountain to the nearest town, Arequipa. There the bundle was painstakingly unwrapped to reveal the body of a girl of about 14, just under 5 feet (1.47 m) tall and, until her sudden death five centuries earlier, in good physical condition.

Reinhard subsequently discovered the bodies of two other children on a small plateau lower down Ampato's slopes; a fourth body was found two years later. Investigation of two nearby peaks, Sara Sara and Pichu Pichu, also yielded evidence of ritual platforms and further child corpses, and Reinhard discovered 10 more in the same general area in 1998–1999. In all, more than two dozen such burials have now been found in southern Peru, northern Chile and northwestern Argentina.

A violent end

Although investigation of the mountain bodies is ongoing, some facts are already clear. The dead were all young, ranging in age from about six to early adulthood. Boys

"Many boys and girls were sacrificed in pairs, being buried alive well dressed and adorned. With each pair they buried ... items that a married Indian possesses."

(Juan de Batanzos, Spanish soldier and chronicler, writing in 1551)

and girls are almost equally represented. Confusingly, their remains are often referred to as "mountain mummies" or "mummy-bundles", but in fact no attempt was made to embalm the corpses. They owe their remarkable state of preservation simply to the extraordinary setting in which they were laid to rest. The cold, dry air of the high Andes helped prevent rapid decay, and snow and ice completed the job of deep-freeze refrigeration.

Medical examination of the corpses has revealed that most of the young victims died by violence, apparently inflicted on the mountaintops. Inspection of the Ampato maiden with the aid of a CT (computed tomography) scanner has revealed that she was killed by a single blow to the right side of the head that fractured her skull and caused a massive haemorrhage. Other victims in the Arequipa region seem to have been killed in similar fashion. Victims found earlier at locations further to the south had reportedly either been buried alive or left to freeze to death. Yet as the Ampato corpse also at first showed no clear sign of trauma, it may be that some of them too had in fact been dispatched, perhaps by strangling, although it is also possible that they were drugged with alcohol or coca leaves and simply abandoned in their mountain tombs.

The ultimate sacrifice

The horror of the mountain graves has come as something of a shock to historians, for the Inca rarely resorted to human sacrifice, avoiding the excesses of the Aztecs and other Mesoamerican cultures that famously sent many thousands of victims to the grave. Yet the idea of sacrifice itself was deeply embedded

below: The Inca often buried tiny figurines with the dead. These gold dolls are dressed in fine textiles – an important sign of wealth and status in Inca society.

in the Inca worldview (see box, right). However, most of the victims were animals, typically guinea-pigs or llamas. Human sacrifice was mostly reserved for very exceptional circumstances, usually involving some great event such as a military victory or the death of a ruler.

Most of the written information on Inca sacrifice comes from hostile sources – mainly Spanish missionaries seeking to uproot the old beliefs – so the reliability of the accounts has often been questioned. For example, when Father Bernabé Cobo wrote in his *Historia del Nuevo Mundo* in 1653 that 200 children were sacrificed to celebrate an emperor's coronation, many historians discounted the report as hostile propaganda, or at least exaggeration.

Similarly, stories of a custom called *capacocha* – a Hispanicization of the Inca phrase *capac hucha*, meaning "royal obligation" – roused some scepticism. According to the chronicles, boys or girls of flawless beauty were led from their native town or village to the Inca capital of Cuzco in ceremonial processions. In the capital they were the focus of parades and ceremonies, after which they were taken back home. There, after further celebrations, they were led to local *huaca*s, or holy places, where they were drugged with *chicha* beer or coca leaves and, once unconscious, offered up as sacrificial victims. Sometimes they were strangled or their throats were cut; others were killed with a blow to the head.

Sacred mountains

The notion of sacred places reached deep into Inca religious life. A *huaca* could be anything that inspired awe and veneration.

left: The mummified body of this young Inca boy, with elaborately braided hair and a feather headdress, was found on the El Pomo peak in Chile. A sacrifice to the gods, he was buried alive on the mountaintop.

Sometimes the objects venerated were manmade – statues or shrines, for example – but normally they were natural features. The chronicler Garcilaso de la Vega (1539–1616), himself half-Inca, spoke of people worshipping plants, flowers, trees, mountains, rocks, caves, precious stones, wild animals and some birds.

Amid the general nature worship, mountains occupied a special place. The Andes were never far away in the Inca lands, and the jagged peaks' snow-capped majesty was as impressive then as it is today; in addition, the thunderstorms that often play about the summits must have increased the sense that they were home to mighty beings. In a generally arid land the mountains were also vital to everyday survival as the source of water: mostly life-giving, in the form of river runoff for drinking and irrigation, but occasionally lethal when heavy rainfall on the peaks caused flash floods.

It is easy, then, to see why people should have regarded the mountains with religious awe; yet, even so, the efforts they made to propitiate the gods that watched over them were extraordinary. The procession that led the Ampato girl to her death must have taken days to reach the mountaintop; the remains of stone shelters found 16,400 and 19,000 feet (5,000 and 5,800 m) up evidently acted as overnight camps or resting-points on the way. Simply carrying the offerings buried with the body and the stones needed to construct

A Gift for the Gods

Before the Spaniards arrived in the New World, the llama was the continent's largest beast of burden. For Andean peoples such as the Inca, the animal had become an integral part of their culture, revered as a provider of food, clothing and labour. Llamas were incorporated into important rituals and were sacrificed to the gods: in Cuzco, a white llama was offered up daily to Inti, the sun god.

The llama's links with the spirit world were potent. Some people said that llamas could see into the future, while others believed that the souls of the dead were sometimes reborn as llamas. Human sacrifices were many times rarer than animal sacrifices, and the chosen victims were honoured and given valuable items to accompany their

above: *This 9-in (22.5-cm) high Inca silver statuette represents a llama wearing a royal blanket decorated with gold and cinnabar.*

immortal soul beyond the grave. One of the images most often buried with them, no doubt in the hope that the gods would send plentiful flocks, was a beautiful figurine of the all-important llama.

the grave, together with the special red earth that lined it, must have been exhausting and dangerous.

Yet the greatest price paid to appease the mountain gods was that demanded of the victims themselves. Whatever steps may have been taken to relieve their suffering, the sheer brutality of their deaths is still disturbing, the more so because Inca society was generally solicitous for

children's welfare, protecting them even before birth (procuring or performing an abortion was punishable by death). Oddly, the high esteem in which children were held may go some way to explain, if not to excuse, the mountain sacrifices. For a devout people, the greatest gifts that they could offer to the gods were the loved ones who were closest to their hearts.

THE EARLIEST EUROPEANS
THE ALPINE ICEMAN
MEGALITHIC TOMBS
THE MOUND PEOPLE
BODIES FROM THE BOGS
ETRUSCAN CITIES OF THE DEAD
THE TOWNS THAT DISAPPEARED
NORTHERN SHIP BURIALS
THE QILAKITSOQ CORPSES

chapter 3

WESTERN EUROPE

Megaliths and Mound-Builders

THE EARLIEST EUROPEANS

Forty thousand years ago, Europe was home to two races – the ancestors of today's humans and the Neanderthals. That much paleontologists can agree on, although much else about the early history of the continent's inhabitants remains controversial – and much of the argument centres on human bones and on burial practices.

There is even doubt over what, scientifically, to call the two races. In recent years they have both normally been regarded as subspecies of the modern human race, *Homo sapiens*, respectively as *Homo sapiens sapiens* and *Homo sapiens neanderthalensis*. Such a labelling implies that the two races could have interbred.

In support of this view, paleontologists have cited a child's skeleton found at Lagar Velho in Portugal. The skeleton, which is around 24,000 years old, combines a skull like that of modern humans with short, sturdy limbs of a type generally associated with the Neanderthals. Opponents of hybridization, however, see the child as nothing more than an unusually stocky example of *Homo sapiens*. For them there remain two distinct species, *Homo sapiens* and *Homo neanderthalensis*.

The disappearance of the Neanderthals

One undisputed fact about the Neanderthals is that they died out as a separate race, disappearing from most of Europe by about 30,000 years ago. They were apparently displaced by modern humans, who arrived in Europe from the east around 42,000 years ago.

At first sight this fact is surprising, for the Neanderthals – so called because their remains were first identified in the Neander valley near Düsseldorf in 1856 – were seemingly well adapted to the continent's special conditions. They had evolved in Europe during the Ice Age, when glaciers reached down almost as far as London and Hamburg. As a result, the Neanderthals were cold-weather specialists, built robustly with the barrel chests, heavy bones and muscular limbs needed to eke a living from the northern tundra; in contrast, the *Homo sapiens* immigrants were used to warmer climes.

Differences in burial customs

What was the special aptitude that enabled modern humans to replace their rivals on their own territory?

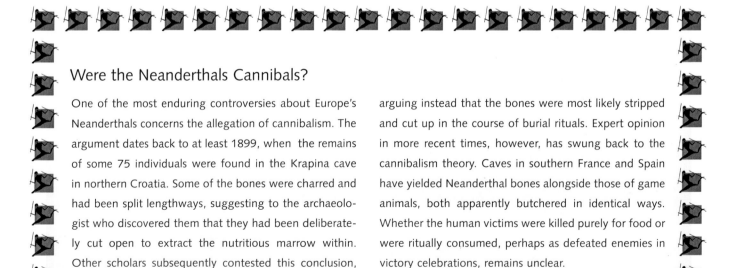

Were the Neanderthals Cannibals?

One of the most enduring controversies about Europe's Neanderthals concerns the allegation of cannibalism. The argument dates back to at least 1899, when the remains of some 75 individuals were found in the Krapina cave in northern Croatia. Some of the bones were charred and had been split lengthways, suggesting to the archaeologist who discovered them that they had been deliberately cut open to extract the nutritious marrow within. Other scholars subsequently contested this conclusion, arguing instead that the bones were most likely stripped and cut up in the course of burial rituals. Expert opinion in more recent times, however, has swung back to the cannibalism theory. Caves in southern France and Spain have yielded Neanderthal bones alongside those of game animals, both apparently butchered in identical ways. Whether the human victims were killed purely for food or were ritually consumed, perhaps as defeated enemies in victory celebrations, remains unclear.

A strong clue may lie in the burial practices of the two groups. It was assumed for several decades after the Neanderthals were first discovered that they simply left their dead to lie where they fell. Then, from 1908 on, reports started to come in, not just from Europe but also from regions as far afield as the former Soviet Union and the Near East, of Neanderthal skeletons that seemed to have been deliberately laid to rest, often accompanied by flint artefacts. In a cave in Uzbekistan, the remains of a young boy were found with the horns of six ibexes apparently arranged in a circle around his head. In Iraq flower pollen was found on one skeleton, suggesting that blossoms had been left on the body rather as modern mourners leave wreaths.

The evidence was occasionally compelling, but also, unfortunately, circumstantial; it is, after all, hardly surprising to find tools, animal remains or even flower pollen in caves in which people lived. In such cases the evidence of intentional burial has to come from the positioning of the objects around the corpse; and it is hard, after a gap of 50,000 years, to be sure whether, say, a hand axe found by a corpse was placed there by mourners as a grave good or was simply something that the deceased had kept at hand, even when dying.

above: The paintings in the Lascaux caves in France are among the best examples of Palaeolithic art. The *Homo sapiens* ancestors of modern Europeans created these images 17,000 years ago.

Probably some Neanderthals did lay their dead to rest, but the case is not definitely proven.

Compare the Neanderthal evidence with that provided by *Homo sapiens* burials, and the difference becomes apparent. Unlike the Neanderthals, the ancestors of modern humans were accomplished artists, as the cave paintings and sculptures of France and Spain show. Artefacts found with their dead include ivory bracelets and beads, shell ornaments and animal-tooth necklaces; even small figurines accompanied one female body found in the Czech Republic. At Sungir in Russia, archaeologists unearthed the skeleton of a man buried in a specially-dug pit filled with red ochre − more than 3,500 ivory beads were found with the body.

The extra elaboration of *Homo sapiens* burials suggests a level of cultural achievement that the Neanderthals never attained. Even though both groups had brains of similar capacity and shared similar lifestyles, it may well have been the newcomers' additional inventiveness and adaptability that ultimately gave them the evolutionary advantage.

THE ALPINE ICEMAN

On 19 September 1991 Helmut and Erika Simon, a German couple, were enjoying a walking holiday in the Tyrol. Having reached the summit of a mountain they were beginning their descent when, in a saddle between two peaks that also served as a high pass between Austria and Italy, they noticed something dark against the snow. As they drew closer, they realized that it was a man's head and shoulders protruding from the melting ice. The pair could not have known it then, but they had stumbled on the traces of the world's most ancient murder mystery.

The Simons duly reported their find to the local authorities, who assumed that the dead person must have been the victim of a long-past mountaineering accident. Five such bodies had already been discovered that summer, as freak weather conditions had brought a fall of wind-borne, heat-absorbing dust from the Sahara that had melted unusual amounts of ice. It was only when investigators started examining objects found around the corpse, including a copper-bladed axe and animal-hide clothing, that some inkling of its true age dawned on them. Even so, no one was prepared for what happened when the body was sent for radiocarbon dating. Analysis of grass samples found with it dated it back to ca. 3300BCE, an era before even the time of the first pharaohs of ancient Egypt. The corpse of the Iceman, as the unknown victim was soon nicknamed, was the oldest well-preserved human body in the world.

Who was the Iceman?

What was the Iceman doing 10,600 feet (3,200 m) up in the Alps when he met his death? Examination showed he was at least 25 years old when he died, and may have reached his late 40s – an advanced age for the time in which he lived, when only one person in 50 reached their 40th year. His body measured about 5 feet, 4 inches (1.6 m) when it was discovered, but might have shrunk as a result of desiccation. Not much DNA was recovered – less than a millionth of the original total –

"The mortal remains of an unknown mountaineer were discovered last Thursday afternoon on the Niederjochferner in the neighbourhood of Söldern. The identity of the corpse, which has been lying in the ice for several decades, has not yet been established."

perhaps because the ice around the body had melted at least once before, causing degradation. What was found, however, corresponded quite closely to the DNA of existing populations in the Alpine region and northern Europe, indicating a remarkable degree of genetic continuity in local populations. Analysis of the contents of the Iceman's colon revealed traces of wheat bread grilled over an open fire, and also pollen from the hop hornbeam, which blooms locally from March to June – suggesting that he had died in spring or early summer. Grains of einkorn wheat found in his colon and on his clothing suggested that he did not live by hunting alone, but also had access to crops.

As might have been expected of an older man in such early times, the Iceman had suffered from various medical conditions, including arthritis, which affected his neck, lower back and right hip, and whipworm, traces of which were found in his intestines. Analysis of a fingernail found detached from the corpse suggested that in the four months preceding his death he had undergone at least three bouts of illness sufficiently serious to interrupt normal growth. No fewer than eight of his ribs had been broken, but the fractures had probably occurred after death as a result of the pressure of ice on the body.

Armed and dressed for the cold

In spite of his various ailments the Iceman, to judge from the state in which his body was found, was still leading an active life. He was well wrapped up against the Alpine cold. He wore a leather loincloth kept in place by a belt of hide that also supported, via garterlike straps, a pair of fur legwarmers. These stretched from the upper thigh to the ankles, where a little tongue of fur served to tuck them into his boots. Another thick fur blanket, held in place by a second belt, was wrapped around his upper body. No trace of coverings for the shoulders or arms were found, but as these were the first parts of the body to become exposed, whatever he was wearing had probably rotted away. Over his other garments he wore a cape of woven straw that could have doubled as a groundsheet or blanket when he chose to rest. To complete his outfit, the Iceman wore leather shoes stuffed with grass for insulation, and a warm cap of bearskin, sewn from several different pieces into a bowl shape and held in place by a leather strap.

Investigators had greater difficulty interpreting the equipment that the Iceman carried with him. There was a lot of it, suggesting that he had set off purposefully on a journey rather than simply heading up into the hills. He seemed kitted out for hunting, for he carried a bow 6 feet (1.8 m) long and a quiver bearing 14 arrows, as well as a small knife with a flint blade. On closer inspection,

below: The Iceman's body was found in melting ice high on the Austro-Italian border. A 12-year dispute between the two countries over ownership of the corpse was resolved in 2003 by a study of minerals from his dental enamel and bone. The results proved that the Iceman spent his whole life in what is now South Tyrol, Italy.

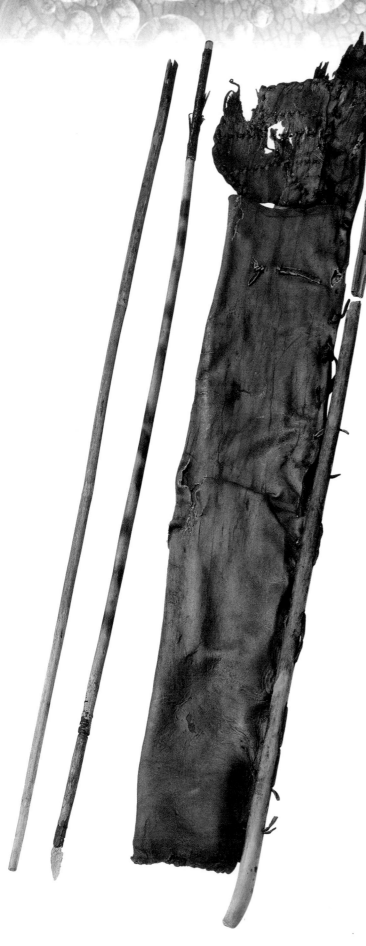

however, 12 of the arrows were found to have no tips. Had the Iceman set off on a hunting trip carrying unfinished equipment?

The most unexpected item of the Iceman's kit was a copper axe, with the blade bound with leather thongs to a yew handle 24 inches (60 cm) long. The surprise lay in the copper blade, for metallurgy was a new technology at the time, and modern scholars had not realized that it had reached the Tyrol so early. Its scarcity would probably have given the axe considerable value. The heavy tool was unlikely to have been of much use on a hunting expedition, and the Iceman's reasons for carrying it remain unclear. Perhaps he used it to haft the shafts of his arrows, or maybe it was simply too precious to leave behind in an unguarded home. To judge from traces of arsenic and other substances involved in the copper-smelting process that were found in his hair, it is even possible that he was himself a metalworker.

How did he die?

The fact that the body was found on a high mountain pass suggested that the Iceman died while moving from one valley to another. His corpse lay in a sheltered gully between parallel rock outcrops – the sort of refuge a traveller might well have chosen in order to sit out a storm. This seemed to suggest an obvious scenario: the Iceman had been caught out by bad weather, and had sought shelter. He was already in frail health, and the conditions had proved too much for him. As a result, he had died of exposure where he lay.

In 2001, however, this straightforward picture was complicated by an unexpected new find. Following its transfer from Innsbruck in Austria to the Italian city of Bolzano, the body was subjected to a new series of examinations. X-rays revealed a crucial detail that had previously been missed: a stone arrowhead embedded in

left: Among the Iceman's equipment was a long bow and this birch-bark quiver that contained 12 unfinished and two finished arrows, which could be used to kill a bear or wolf – or another person.

the Iceman's shoulder. Examination of the entry point suggested that it was a fresh wound, inflicted shortly before his death, that had not had time to heal.

Further examinations a few months later revealed that the Iceman had suffered serious injuries to his right hand and wrist caused by a sharp object, perhaps a flint dagger, apparently during hand-to-hand combat shortly before his death. If such was the case, then the Iceman must have known that he was in danger and tried to defend himself. Could he have been ambushed?

The Iceman fought back

A year after the discovery of the hand and wrist injuries, fresh research cast new light on the Iceman's last hours. Molecular biologist Thomas Loy led a team that studied DNA samples taken from some of the Iceman's tools, weapons and clothing, using techniques devised specifically for working with ancient DNA. To their surprise, the investigators found blood from four different people.

Based on the evidence they uncovered, Loy devised his own theory of how the Iceman died. He believes that he was hunting high in the Alps with at least one companion when he wandered into territory controlled by another group and became involved in a skirmish. The Iceman shot at least two people with his bow, each time retrieving the arrow in order to re-use it. He then missed a target and the arrow broke. Perhaps while trying to defend himself in hand-to-hand combat, he was shot with an arrow from behind, but managed to get away, heading up the mountainside. Traces of another person's blood on the shoulder of his leather jacket suggest that he may have carried a wounded companion for a distance. Loy also found that the Iceman's arrow wound had been stitched; presumably the same companion, or else a third individual, removed the arrow shaft from his back, leaving the head behind, and then performed makeshift surgery.

All these discoveries have put a new complexion on the Iceman's final hours. Now it would seem that he was on the run from enemies when his strength gave way. Losing blood, and probably suffering from an infection from the shoulder wound, he managed to clamber almost all the way up the slope. Just before the descent his strength gave way. Maybe he sat down to rest, or perhaps he collapsed; either way, the cold of the high peaks finished off the work that an act of violence had begun hours or days before.

Evidence of Early Acupuncture?

Ever since the first discovery of the Iceman's body, people have speculated about several groups of bluish-black marks visible on the corpse's lower back and legs. Early witnesses mistook them for the brands once used to scar criminals, but they are now known to be tattoos, probably made by forcing charcoal soot into the skin with some form of needle. In all, 15 separate sets have been discovered, some of them only visible under infra-red light. Most are on parts of the body that would normally have been covered by clothing, so it seems unlikely that they were intended for decoration. Investigators have pointed out that most were found at spots liable to aches and pains – the lower back, joints, knees and ankles – leading to speculation that they might have been meant to have a therapeutic effect. Research subsequently showed that nine of the 15 fall either on or within 0.2 inches (5 mm) of traditional Chinese acupuncture points, suggesting that early Europeans might have had some knowledge of pressure points and have sought relief, magical or otherwise, by probing them.

MEGALITHIC TOMBS

Few ancient structures have mystified and fascinated people over so many years as the megalithic monuments of western Europe. The word "megalith" comes from the Greek for "big stone", and is used to describe menhirs, such as the one at Locmariaquer in Brittany; stone circles, including the famous rings at Avebury in England, or rows, such as those at Carnac in Brittany; and "temples", the best known being England's Stonehenge. Much of the mystery of the megaliths stems from the total absence of written sources for the period in which they were built. Recently archaeology has begun to provide some basis for rational speculation about how and why the gigantic constructions were erected. It is the megalith builders' tombs, many of which also incorporate large stones in their structure, that provide the most clues about the way of life of the people who erected these enigmatic monuments.

Megaliths and social change

Thanks to radiocarbon dating of organic deposits found in conjunction with the stones, scholars now know that the tombs and monuments were constructed ca. 4700–1800BCE in the Neolithic period – the New Stone Age. This was a time of massive social change, when Europe was undergoing the greatest revolution it had known since the arrival of the first *Homo sapiens* hunter-gatherers: the birth of agriculture. Farming spread westward from the Middle East from around 7000BCE on. Its progress was slow, however, and at least three millennia were to pass before agriculture became Europe's main source of food.

Many scholars now link the phenomenon of megalith-building with the spread of farming, but the way in which the two were connected remains controversial. The upsurge in stone construction seems to have coincided with the arrival of people bringing with them the new methods of cultivation – a group known as the Linear Pottery people, from the style of ceramics found in their graves. The main concentration of megalithic remains lies in the Atlantic lands, from Spain and Portugal northward to Scandinavia, including mainland Britain and Ireland. These regions were also the ones where Europe's old hunter-gatherer population was most heavily concentrated. So, the megaliths went up in the region where the conflict of lifestyles was most marked; what part they played in the ensuing culture clash is hard to determine because of the general uncertainty about the functions they performed.

right: Gavrinis tomb, a large tumulus which stands on an island off the Brittany coast, is an example of a passage grave.

Stone chambers for the dead

Megalithic tombs consisted of artificial burial chambers created by using large, table-shaped stones that were then covered over with substantial earth mounds. Most such structures were clearly built to serve as receptacles for individual or mass burials. Yet opinion remains divided over

the primary function of some of the bigger, more complex structures, such as the megalithic passage tombs in Ireland's Boyne Valley (including Newgrange, see overleaf).

Dolmens, as megalithic tombs are often called, are found across Europe, but they were first studied in detail in England. Early British antiquaries learned to distinguish two types: those that were roughly circular in shape under their earth covering and that usually contained only a single burial chamber (called "round barrows") and those that were elongated, which typically contained the bones of many individuals ("long barrows"). Later investigators would divide the long barrows into passage graves, in which a stone passage led to a burial chamber, and gallery graves, in which there was no burial chamber and the interments took place in the passage itself.

The first major breakthrough in interpreting the tombs was made in the 1850s by an English amateur archaeologist named John Thurnam. He did pioneering work on barrows in the southern county of Wiltshire, deducing, correctly, that the long barrows were older than the round barrows. He also noted that the occupants of the long barrows were never buried with metal artefacts, while those of the round barrows

left: Newgrange in Ireland (ca. 3200BCE) was built to align with the sunrise on the winter solstice, when the sun's rays fill the mound's passage and central chamber. The structure was probably a ceremonial, astrological and religious centre as well as a tomb.

often were. Finally, he took to measuring the skulls that he found in the two types of tomb. He determined that long barrows contained almost exclusively dolichocephalic (long, narrow) skulls, and round barrows brachycephalic (broad, round) skulls.

Subsequent discoveries have indicated that two different cultures, probably involving separate ethnic groups, were responsible for the two types of grave. The long barrows, which date back as far as 4500BCE in Brittany and to about 4000BCE in Britain, are thought to have been spread by the Linear Pottery farmers, who used stone tools and practised an egalitarian lifestyle. A typical long barrow contained the bones of several individuals jumbled together in democratic anonymity.

An early elite

Round barrows, in contrast, are particularly associated with the Beaker Culture, a later development deriving its name from the waisted drinking vessels that were its hallmark. The Beaker people were metalworkers – the first to bring the new skill to the continent's western margins. Their heyday, ca. 2500–200BCE, saw something of a revolution in social customs. While the

"We had opened up a long gallery filled almost to the top with stones, to arrive eventually at the heart of the monument. It was breathtaking. The *tholos* [beehive-shaped] structure was intact. The circular vault was glistening with a myriad of faceted, shimmering beads: drops of water which had condensed on the schist and granite capstones – an unforgettable moment in an archaeologist's career!"

(French archaeologist Jacques Briard, describing the opening in 1955 of a Breton long barrow containing 11 separate circular burial chambers)

The Amesbury Archer

Archaeologists have recently discovered a grave located 3 miles (5 km) from Stonehenge and dating to around the time the giant monument was being constructed (ca. 2300BCE). The occupant was laid to rest alongside an amazing hoard of more than 100 objects, including clothing, Beaker pots, flints, boar tusks, copper knives, two gold earrings (see right) and two gold hair tresses. Discovered in 2002, the body has been nicknamed the "Amesbury Archer" because the skeleton wore a slate wristguard to protect the arm from the recoil of

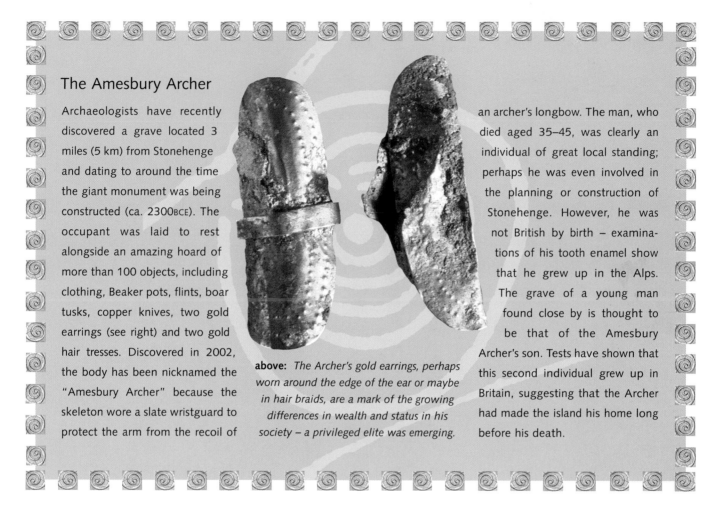

above: *The Archer's gold earrings, perhaps worn around the edge of the ear or maybe in hair braids, are a mark of the growing differences in wealth and status in his society – a privileged elite was emerging.*

an archer's longbow. The man, who died aged 35–45, was clearly an individual of great local standing; perhaps he was even involved in the planning or construction of Stonehenge. However, he was not British by birth – examinations of his tooth enamel show that he grew up in the Alps. The grave of a young man found close by is thought to be that of the Amesbury Archer's son. Tests have shown that this second individual grew up in Britain, suggesting that the Archer had made the island his home long before his death.

Neolithic farmers had shared the fruits of the earth, the precious new copper and bronze artefacts concentrated wealth in the hands of a few.

In the early Bronze Age world of the Beaker people, possessions assumed a new importance. Privileged individuals could amass fortunes by owning scarce metal goods, while copper or bronze weapons gave them power. Such people expected privileged treatment in life and in death, and their leaders were often buried alone. Typically, they chose to face eternity surrounded by expensive grave goods. The occupant of one

barrow, just over a mile (1.6 km) from Stonehenge, was laid to rest alongside two copper daggers, a bronze axe, a bronze-tipped lance and a dagger sheath inlaid with thousands of tiny gold pins.

The Beaker Culture barrows were not just a British phenomenon; burial sites similar to the ones Thurnam studied have been found all the way from Ireland to Poland. Recently, fresh evidence that the new style arrived from the continent along with the skills of metalworking has emerged in the so-called Amesbury Archer's burial (see box, above):

among the archer's grave goods were copper knives from Spain and France.

Another metalworking tradition, known as the Corded Ware Culture, left a second trail of distinctive pottery and metal goods in similar mounds stretching from Scandinavia to central Russia. Four thousand years on, the tumuli built by these Beaker and Corded Ware metalsmiths still bear witness to one of Europe's greatest social revolutions – a change that would see communally-minded Neolithic villagers give way to the Bronze Age warrior-aristocrats familiar from the pages of Homer.

THE MOUND PEOPLE

Since well before Viking times, the fields of Denmark's Jutland peninsula have been punctuated by low mounds, often sited in high places where they dominate the landscape. In all there are more than 300 of them, averaging 60 feet (18 m) across and 10 feet (3 m) in height, although some are much bigger. Most were constructed around 1300BCE, a period that seems to have been something of a golden age in which Jutland's inhabitants earned a comfortable living primarily as farmers and rearers of livestock.

Memorials to the dead

Similar mounds, dating from ca. 3000BCE on, are found elsewhere in Europe and have generally been associated with the burials of Bronze Age chieftains. Danish mounds, however, form a particularly close-knit group, most having been erected within a century or two of one another.

The Jutland mounds were raised over the graves of men and women buried in their everyday clothes, yet accompanied by weapons and ornaments elegantly fashioned from gold and bronze. To judge from their contents, this was an ordered, relatively affluent culture, linked by trade networks to lands far away.

The Sun Chariot

In September 1902 a farmer ploughing boggy land at Trundholm on the Danish island of Zealand turned up an object that cast a ray of light on the mound builders' religious beliefs. When reassembled, the object turned out to be an image of the sun pulled by a bronze horse (see illustration, right); a rolled-up piece of paper-thin gold foil found nearby fitted across one face of the solar disc. Horse and sun were both set on wheels, probably so that the model could be pulled in ritual processions.

Although little is known of the beliefs of Bronze Age Scandinavia, the idea of horses drawing the sun across the sky is common to many mythologies, including that of ancient Greece. The myth most likely originated with the Indo-Europeans, famed horsemen who invaded India in the second millennium BCE and also spread out over much of Europe.

The people of Bronze Age Denmark must have had time on their hands given the amount of work that went into raising the mounds. They were built of layers of turf, sometimes buttressed by rings of stones; scholars believe that it would have taken the top cover of 2.5–3.7 acres (1–1.5 hectares) of good pasture land to build one. Saturated by the rain of centuries, the peat helped preserve the log coffins in which the dead were laid to rest, much as it did the celebrated bog bodies of northern Europe (see pages 82–5). In the mounds, however, acidic water seeping into the coffins mostly ate away the skeletons inside, often leaving hair, brains, fingernails and jawbones as the only recognizable human remains. Textiles and metals fared much better.

Several dozen such coffins have been recovered over the past two centuries. Most contained the bodies of sword-bearing males, presumably local chieftains. In life they seem to have been healthy and well-nourished, averaging 5 feet, 7 inches (1.72 m) in height. The dead wore long woollen tunics and thick woollen caps covered in knotted threads, thought to have helped ward off sword blows in battle.

The Egtved girl

The bodies of several women have also been found. The most remarkable discovery came in 1921, when a farmer levelling a mound at Egtved in southern Jutland came upon an oak coffin containing the remains of a girl of about 20. Although the bones had mostly dissolved, the shape of the body was still visible, and the girl's shoulder-length hair and carefully tended fingernails had survived. So too had her clothes, and these proved a major surprise. The Egtved girl had been buried wearing a short-sleeved woollen tunic, a belt supporting a bronze disc covering her otherwise bare midriff, and a corded miniskirt just 16 inches (40 cm) long. The outfit looked startlingly modern.

Other aspects of the burial brought the circumstances of the entombment remarkably close. A brownish deposit in the coffin turned out to be the dried remains of the funeral drink, an alcoholic concoction of wheat and cranberries sweetened with honey and spiced with bog myrtle. There was also a sprig of flowering yarrow; dropped in the coffin by a mourner, it showed that the last rites had taken place in summer. A more sinister find was a bundle containing the cremated bones of a girl of about nine, thought to be a servant sacrificed to accompany her mistress into the afterlife.

BODIES FROM THE BOGS

In the years of austerity following the Second World War, peat was much in demand in Denmark as a cheap source of fuel. Sometimes the cutters working in the remote and lonely bogs where it lay found more than just the damp, compacted moss itself.

One such event took place on 8 May 1950. Two men digging near Tollund in central Jutland came upon the remains of a body. They alerted the authorities, who immediately suspected that the corpse might be an ancient one – over the centuries, dozens or even hundreds such had been found in bogs and fens across Denmark – and notified the archaeologist Peter Glob. The body was quickly exhumed; Glob, meanwhile, would go on to write a classic history of the bog people.

Macabre discoveries

On examination, the corpse turned out to be that of a man aged between 40 and 50, about 5 feet, 4 inches (1.6 m) in height. He was naked but for a leather belt and a conical sheepskin cap. His face bore an extraordinary expression of serenity, as though he were only sleeping – an impression quickly dispelled when a sod of turf was removed to reveal a rope around his neck. Subsequent investigation indicated that it had been tightened relatively slowly – none of the vertebrae had broken – suggesting that Tollund Man had been garrotted rather than hanged. Carbon-14 dating showed that he had met his death around 210BCE.

Two years later a similarly gruesome discovery was made at Grauballe, about 12 miles (20 km) from Tollund. Again, the body was that of a naked man, this one in his early 30s. This time there was no ambiguity about the cause of death: the man's throat had been cut from ear to ear. The corpse was well enough preserved to allow fingerprints to be taken, and the pattern of loops and whorls proved similar to that of many Danish people today. Carbon dating allowed researchers to date the body to ca. 55BCE.

Thanks partly to Glob's book (*The Bog People; Iron Age Man Preserved*, first published in 1969), Tollund and Grauballe Man are now two of the best-known examples of a phenomenon – that of bog bodies – that has intrigued and disturbed people for centuries. Such bodies are not limited to Denmark, although it has an unusually high number – they are also found all across northern Europe, from Ireland to Poland. In all, about 1,800 have been identified, with the greatest numbers coming, after Denmark, from Germany, Britain and the Netherlands. Only a small percentage have been dated reliably, but of those that have the majority died between 500BCE and 500CE, in the late Bronze and Iron Ages. However, the earliest body dates back to 10,000BCE, deep into the Stone Age, and a few bodies from more recent times have also been recovered.

"There is a strange power in bog water that prevents decay. Bodies have been found that must have lain in bogs for more than a thousand years, but which, although admittedly rather shrunken and brown, are in other respects unchanged."

(EXCERPT FROM AN 1837 DANISH ALMANAC, COMMENTING ON THE DISCOVERY OF A WOMAN'S BODY IN HARALDSKJAER FEN TWO YEARS EARLIER)

One point about which there is no mystery is the reason for the bodies' excellent preservation. The peat bogs are primarily composed of compressed sphagnum moss which, as it decays, gives off sufficient humic acid to kill most of the bacteria that cause decomposition. If concentration levels are right, both skin and bones survive; however, a high acid content can dissolve the bones while still preserving the flesh, which turns brown like leather. The cold weather of northern climes also helps, slowing decomposition when the body sinks, as does the lack of oxygen in the bogs' lower depths.

Victims of a violent death

There are obviously many ways in which bodies could have found their way into bogs in such varied lands over so many centuries. Some victims may have fallen in accidentally; others may have been deliberately buried. Most attention, however, has focused on the Bronze and Iron Age bodies, which show some intriguing common features. One is the signs of violence found on many

of the corpses. Besides garrotting and throat cutting, victims have been found stabbed to death or killed by blows to the head. Other victims were apparently pegged down in the marsh and left to drown. Severed heads have also been discovered.

Further peculiarities mark out these finds. Most of the bodies were naked, like Tollund and Grauballe Man, and several of the women had their heads wholly or partially shaved. Men and women are almost equally represented among the victims, but there are more young people and adults in the prime of life than might have been expected from a random sample of the population; relatively few children's bodies have been found. Many of the victims seem to have come from privileged backgrounds – they were robust and well-nourished in life and their hands and fingernails show few signs of manual labour. The number of physically handicapped individuals is also unusually high; bodies have been found showing signs of scoliosis (curvature of the spine), spina bifida, osteoporosis, stunted limbs, and damaged hips that would have caused limping. One victim had vestigial extra thumbs.

Punishment or sacrifice?

Such findings have caused much speculation about the reasons behind the killings. Two main schools of thought have developed, respectively involving punishment and sacrifice. One points to almost the only extensive

left: Tollund Man, whose manner of death was characteristic of the threefold ritual killing that formed part of Celtic tradition: the smashing of the skull, garrotting of the neck and cutting of the throat. It suggests that Celtic practices had reached non-Celtic speakers.

written source on the northern lands in the Iron Age: the *Germania* ("About Germany") of the Roman historian Tacitus (ca. 54–117CE). Tacitus specified that it was the custom of the Germanic tribes to hang traitors and deserters from trees; but cowards, people with no will to fight and sex offenders were "plunged into marshes with hurdles over their heads". In early medieval times, the laws of the Burgundians – a Germanic people – specified that women who were unfaithful to their husbands should die in swamps.

Some people have cavilled at this evidence, pointing out that it postdates most of the bodies and that, in Tacitus's case, it was relayed at second or third hand. These scholars prefer to make a connection between the bodies and the well-established contemporary tradition, usually considered more Celtic than Germanic, of leaving offerings

above: A detail of a man's head from the Gundestrup Cauldron, 1st century BCE, retrieved from a peat bog in Denmark. This large silver bowl had been dismantled before being placed in the bog, possibly as a votive offering. One intriguing scene on the cauldron portrays what appears to be a ritual killing. The cauldron is also decorated with Celtic mythical scenes and deities, including the antler god, and may have reached Denmark as booty from a raid.

in water – the Celts had great reverence for their natural surroundings, especially rivers, streams, lakes and marshes. Among the well-known British offertory sites is Flag Fen in East Anglia, where more than 300 objects, including valuable bronze swords, have been found thrown into marshes. In Fisherton in Lincolnshire a fragment of a man's skull, wounded by a heavy blade, was discovered alongside weapons, pots, tools and ornaments. In

Lindow Man

Outside Denmark, the world's best-known bog body is probably Lindow Man, whose remains are now on display in the British Museum in London. The body first came to light in August 1984, when peat-cutters working in Lindow Moss, a bog in the English county of Cheshire, found a human foot. Further investigation turned up the head and torso of a man who proved on examination to have been dead for almost 2,000 years.

Lindow Man had met a violent death: he had been struck twice on the head with a relatively blunt instrument – each blow had been forceful enough to fracture his skull. He had then been garrotted; as with Tollund Man, the cord was still in position around his neck. In addition, his throat was slit open, although some authorities think that this injury might have been caused posthumously by people digging in the bog. In his 20s or early 30s, about 5 feet, 7 inches (1.7m) tall and in good physical shape, he had been thrown into the bog naked but for a fox-fur amulet around his upper arm. He had neatly-kept nails, indicative of someone not involved in manual labour, and a beard that had been carefully trimmed shortly before his death. The evidence suggested that in life he had been a person of some consequence.

The fact that he died at about the time of the Roman invasion of Britain has led to suggestions that Lindow Man might have been sacrificed by Druids seeking divine assistance against the invaders; but the limited information available means that such theories must remain intriguing speculations.

Denmark, the Trundholm Chariot (see box, page 80) and the Gundestrup Cauldron (see illustration, opposite), two of the nation's best-known ancient artefacts, were both found deposited in bogs. A lingering remnant of this old tradition survives in the custom of throwing coins into fountains for luck.

In this context, it is easy to make the case that the bog bodies were actually sacrificial victims. Tacitus lends weight to this view, too; he wrote of the cult of a goddess named Nerthus, whose image was kept on a wagon in a sacred grove on an island. From time to time the wagon made a ceremonial progress through the countryside. As the goddess passed, all warfare ceased and there was general rejoicing. Once the image returned home, wagon, image and priest were all bathed ritually in a nearby lake, while the servants who had ministered to them were thrown into the waters to drown. Archaeological evidence supporting Tacitus's story has come in the form of two splendidly carved wooden wagons that have been retrieved from bogs. One of the scenes on the Gundestrup Cauldron also appears to hint at human sacrifice. The image shows a god holding a man head down over a bowl, as if to drain his blood into a receptacle not unlike the cauldron itself.

It is, of course, possible that both theories could be right. Conceivably, people condemned to execution – and maybe also individuals whose physical disabilities marked them out as different and separated them from the rest of the community – were selected for sacrifice. In his commentaries, Julius Caesar noted that the gods of the Gauls – a more southerly, Celtic people – liked to be offered criminals, but that if none were available innocent people were sacrificed instead.

Pollen analysis and examination of the stomach contents of some of the better-known bog bodies have shown that the victims were probably killed late in winter and in early spring. Maybe, as Peter Glob himself suggested, these individuals were offered up in fertility rites celebrating the change of the seasons, encouraging the growth of new life by the sacrifice, voluntary or otherwise, of their own.

ETRUSCAN CITIES OF THE DEAD

In ancient times, when Rome was still a small provincial town, the region of Italy now known as Tuscany was inhabited by a people called the Etruscans. Tusci, the root of the word "Tuscany", was one of the names by which their Roman conquerors and successors knew them. Thanks to the riches discovered in their tombs, the Etruscans' mysterious, complex belief system is still intriguing modern scholars, just as it intrigued the Romans before them.

Wealth and influence

In its heyday in the sixth and fifth centuries BCE Etruria was a very prosperous land. Much of the wealth came from its mines, which at the time were the principal source of copper and iron ore in the central Mediterranean area. Traders from Greece and the Greek colonies in southern Italy, as well as from Carthage on the North African coast and from the Mediterranean's eastern seaboard, flocked to the Etruscan ports to exchange luxury goods for the precious ore. The Greeks in particular were to have a crucial influence on their trading partners, passing on to them not just artistic styles and techniques but also knowledge of the alphabet and writing. The Etruscans in turn handed on literacy to their southern neighbours, the Romans – and so to much of the modern world.

Yet, for all their knowledge of letters, the Etruscans left few written records. Most of their books were copied on perishable linen. Only one has survived; it found its way in ancient times to Egypt, where it was re-used as mummy-cloth, only to be miraculously rediscovered in the nineteenth century when the mummy around which it was wound was taken to a museum in Zagreb, Croatia. However, the text turned out to be a dry calendar of religious rituals, and added little to scholars' knowledge of the Etruscan tongue.

Reading the tombs

In the absence of literary texts, investigators have been forced to puzzle out the Etruscans' attitudes to life and to death from the inscriptions, paintings and objects found in the remarkable Etruscan tombs located throughout Tuscany. Ever since classical times, hidden riches have been sporadically unearthed in the region. In the eighteenth century, when a fashion for antiquities stimulated new interest in the tombs, it became apparent just how rich the Etruscan heritage was.

In 1726 the Etruscan Academy was established to investigate the ancient culture. Two years later excavations began at the cliff-top necropolis of Volterra, 30 miles (50 km) southwest of Florence. Soon connoisseurs across Europe were wondering at the finely-sculpted urns and "Etruscan vases" – many of them actually made in Greece – that found their way onto the art market from the diggings. A vogue for all things Etruscan rapidly spread across the continent. When Josiah Wedgwood started building his famous pottery-factory village in the English county of Staffordshire in 1768, he called the site "Etruria" in a nod to the trend.

By any standard, the Volterra tombs themselves were extraordinary. Hollowed out of the soft volcanic rock of the Tuscan country-

left: An Etruscan bronze votive statuette of the kind often found among grave goods portrays a helmeted warrior, his bodily form in a distinctively elongated style.

above: The household items moulded on the walls of the famous Etruscan Tomb of the Reliefs include a handbag and perfume bottle as well as kitchen equipment such as a pestle and rolling-pin.

side, they were designed as comfortable living quarters for the affluent dead. In a typical tomb, a long, sloping passage, known as the *dromos*, with two smaller vestibules giving off on either side, led to a spacious main chamber. At the rear, doors and sometimes windows opened onto other, smaller rooms. The walls were plastered with a mixture of calcium carbonate and clay, providing a smooth surface for decoration. On this neutral ground, Etruscan artists painted the extraordinary, colourful scenes of daily life 2,500 years ago that are the chief glory of the tombs to the present day.

A luxurious afterlife

In the Etruscan prime, people's expectations of the afterlife seem to have been extraordinarily optimistic. The lifelike images adorning the sarcophagi show reclining couples smiling and holding hands – even embracing – as if in expectation of an eternal version of the sumptuous banquets their artists liked to depict on

"I was so much startled as to shrink back; for, the moment the door was opened, the stern, dignified, and colossal visage of an Etruscan chief stared me in the face. He looked as if he had just raised his head from the placid, majestic repose in which he lay."

(ENGLISH TRAVELLER LADY CAROLINE HAMILTON GRAY IN 1839, ON FIRST SIGHTING A TARQUINIAN TOMB MONUMENT MODELLED ON ITS OCCUPANT)

the tomb walls. The dead went to the grave apparently intending to carry on enjoying the good, prosperous life they had known on Earth.

With their eternal comfort in mind, they took care to take with them into the tomb all the equipment needed to maintain their standard of living. One celebrated architectural find, the Tomb of the Reliefs (see illustration, page 87), had carved on its walls and pillars three-dimensional models of the entire contents of a well-equipped household – even a toothed wheel of the type now familiar to us for cutting pasta. There were images of domestic pets too, including dogs and a goose. All, presumably, were designed to serve their owners' enjoyment in the life to come.

The world reflected in the tomb paintings is one of luxurious ease, no doubt because only the rich could afford such extravagance in death. Men and women mix together in easy familiarity at lavish banquets, the womenfolk showing none of the retiring timidity expected of their Greek and Roman counterparts in classical times.

Other scenes show other pleasures. Lissom dancers move gracefully to the sound of lyres, zithers, trumpets and pipes. Jugglers juggle and acrobats entertain. Spectators attend chariot races and sports contests featuring wrestling and boxing, as well as athletic events that include foot races, jumping and discus-throwing. Always the atmosphere is one of grace and pleasure, exemplified by the elegant clothing of the participants, who favoured elaborately decorated robes and headgear, and footwear that included gold-laced sandals and stylish laced leather shoes with upturned toes.

right: A sarcophagus, ca, 4th century BCE, in the form of a banqueting couch with a reclining couple shown at ease together, and presumably representing man and wife. The Etruscans practised both cremation and inhumation (burial), but inhumation remained the traditional funerary rite in the south. Many cinerary urns (containers for the cremated remains of the dead) resemble sarcophoguses in form.

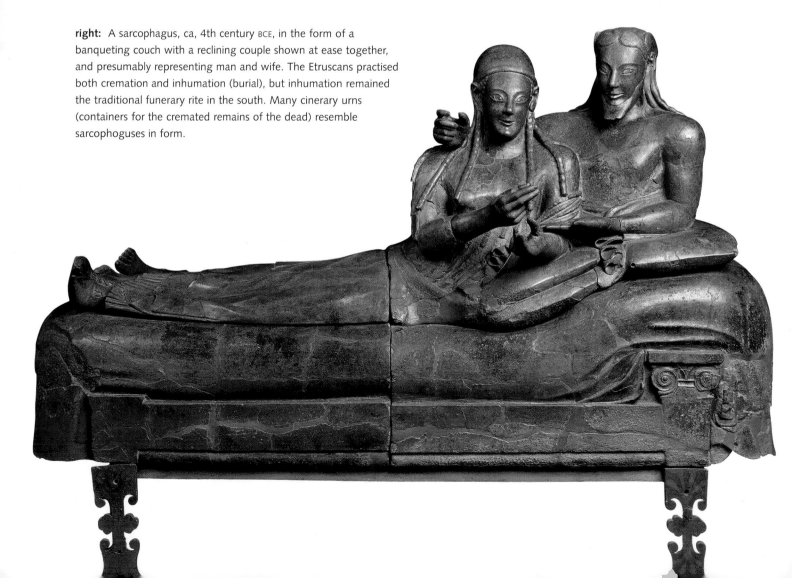

A new pessimism

From the fifth century BCE on, however, the Etruscan world began to change. Roman power was on the rise, and one by one the city-states of Etruria accepted the overlordship of their aggressive southern neighbours. By 89BCE, when Roman citizenship was conferred on all Etruscans, even their language – a mysterious tongue, unrelated to any known family – was falling into disuse, replaced by the ubiquitous Latin.

Changing political fortunes seem to have left their mark on the Etruscan attitude to death. The tombs built in these later centuries of declining power and affluence show a gradual loss of the old *joie de vivre*. While the standard of the artwork remained technically high, the mood darkened, and a new concern with demons and bodily decay came to supplement, if not entirely replace, the old view of the afterlife as a perpetual feast.

Some scholars see the influence of Greek mythology in the change. Certainly Charon, the grim ferryman who transported souls across the Styx to the underworld, crossed over into local beliefs, Etruscanized as Charun and transformed into a sinister figure bearing a mallet. But other death deities that haunted the popular imagination were purely Etruscan, especially the winged goddess Vanth, who bore a torch and a key to unlock tombs, and the demoness Tuchulcha, represented with a vulture's beak, donkey's ears and gorgonesque snakes for hair.

The Tomb of the Blue Demons

Symptomatic of the new mood was the Tomb of the Blue Demons, discovered in 1986 beneath a road in Tarquinia, north of Rome. The tomb was one of more than two dozen found during the construction of a new water main and subsequently investigated with photographic probes; the ones that looked interesting were then excavated.

Dated to around 400BCE, the Tomb of the Blue Demons is transitional. One wall shows the traditional banquet and hunting scenes, but the other reveals a much darker vision. Charun is there, still shown at this early date as the ferryman of Greek legend. Waiting on

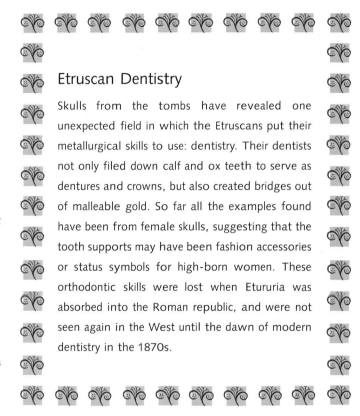

Etruscan Dentistry

Skulls from the tombs have revealed one unexpected field in which the Etruscans put their metallurgical skills to use: dentistry. Their dentists not only filed down calf and ox teeth to serve as dentures and crowns, but also created bridges out of malleable gold. So far all the examples found have been from female skulls, suggesting that the tooth supports may have been fashion accessories or status symbols for high-born women. These orthodontic skills were lost when Etururia was absorbed into the Roman republic, and were not seen again in the West until the dawn of modern dentistry in the 1870s.

the underworld's shore are some human figures, themselves no doubt newly arrived, but also two fearsome demons; one grasps twin serpents, while the other rushes forward menacingly, his lips curled into a snarl and his eyes glowing like embers.

Some scholars view the demons as guardians of the dead rather than their tormentors; their like are sometimes shown protecting the entrances to tombs, as though on sentry duty between the worlds of the dead and the living. Even so, such figures hardly reflected a reassuring picture of the afterlife – their expressions spoke of terrors rather than comforts beyond the grave.

Even after the Roman conquest, the Etruscan heritage lived on in the rites and customs that it bequeathed to the victors. One such was a taste for prophecy: Spurrina, the augur who warned Julius Caesar to beware the ides of March, was Etruscan. Yet the other special qualities of Etruscan civilization were subsumed into the imperial culture of Rome and largely lost, not to be rediscovered for almost 2,000 years.

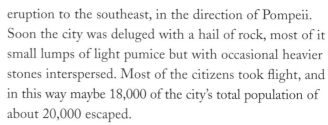

THE TOWNS THAT DISAPPEARED

The disaster that overwhelmed the prosperous Roman towns of Pompeii and Herculaneum in 79CE happened partly in slow motion. Although there had been earlier tremors from Mount Vesuvius, the volcano that dominated both communities, the first serious sign of trouble came around noon on 24 August. Abruptly, the plug of lava that had been blocking the mountain's throat shot high into the heavens. A mushroom cloud spread ominously across the sky. Stratospheric winds carried the debris from the eruption to the southeast, in the direction of Pompeii. Soon the city was deluged with a hail of rock, most of it small lumps of light pumice but with occasional heavier stones interspersed. Most of the citizens took flight, and in this way maybe 18,000 of the city's total population of about 20,000 escaped.

The other 2,000 chose to sit out the storm in their houses or workplaces – a fatal error. Throughout the day and into the night the volcano continued to spew forth rocks. The streets of Pompeii were soon filled with a rising tide of rubble. The *coup de grâce* came in the form of hot

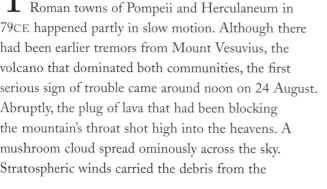

"We had scarcely sat down to rest when darkness fell, not the dark of a moonless or cloudy night, but as if the lamp had been put out in a closed room. You could hear the shrieks of women, the wailing of infants, and the shouting of men; some were calling their parents, others their children or wives, trying to recognize them by their voices. People bewailed their own fate, and there were some who prayed for death in their terror of dying."

(THE ROMAN WRITER PLINY THE YOUNGER, WHO WAS ON THE OPPOSITE SIDE OF THE BAY OF NAPLES FROM POMPEII WHEN VESUVIUS ERUPTED)

left: The plaster cast of a man's body, discovered in Pompeii. He died crouching, undoubtedly in fear, and trying to protect his nose and mouth from the fatal, foul-smelling toxic gases that swept so devastatingly through the town.

clouds of poisonous gas and ash that swept repeatedly through the city and the surrounding countryside, suffocating those in their path. In contrast, Herculaneum was destroyed within minutes, swallowed up by an avalanche of boiling lava as much as 80 feet (25 m) deep. By the time the eruptions finally subsided almost 24 hours after they had begun, the two towns had vanished, smothered under a blanket of hardening lava.

Rediscovery

Herculaneum and Pompeii remained hidden beneath a thick layer of solidified lava for almost 17 centuries. In 1738 investigators, piqued by the intellectual curiosity of the early Enlightenment, determined to penetrate the towns' mysteries. It was to be another 16 years before any proper attempt was made to record the excavations and the artefacts discovered; in the meantime many objects were taken for private collections. Nevertheless, the uncovering of Pompeii and Herculaneum was a pioneering venture that can be said to have marked the beginning

above: The first peristyle courtyard in Pompeii's House of the Faun, so called because of the statue of a dancing faun that adorns the atrium's pool. This was one of the city's largest and most luxurious private houses, featuring lavish wall-paintings and floor mosaics.

of the age of archaeology; nothing like it had ever been tried before, and the project continues to this day.

What the diggers unearthed were the remains of two communities trapped, as though in freeze-frame, when their inhabitants went about their everyday lives. Meals were left unfinished on tables; bread remained half-cooked in bakers' ovens; grass that had just been cut was left lying on lawns. Over the decades, the excavations were to provide an unrivalled flow of information on the minutiae of daily life in Roman provincial towns.

Casting the dead

The human aspect of the disaster only began to become apparent when an archaeologist found a way of recreating the perished remains of those who had died under the rubble. He did so by pouring liquid plaster of Paris into the cavities left where the corpses had decayed. What emerged when the encasing lava was chipped away were plaster casts of the dead as they had fallen. This was a new view of death in the ancient world: raw and naked, with none of the pomp and circumstance of funerary rites or burial. The Pompeiian casts revealed death unposed.

Some of the individuals brought to light in this way had apparently met their fate with resignation. One man seemed to be sleeping, his head resting peacefully on his forearm and his eyes closed. A beggar lay beside the sack in which he had been collecting alms; on his feet were a pair of incongruously elegant sandals, no doubt a gift from some wealthy benefactor.

Other people had been struck down while trying to flee. A servant died as he led a mother and her two sons toward safety; in his hand was the bag in which he had salvaged provisions from the wreckage of his household. One individual had sought refuge from the rising carpet of rubble by climbing a tree; he was captured for posterity with the snapped branch to which he had been clinging still firmly gripped between his legs.

Everywhere there were vignettes of horror and suffering. A terrified dog had scrabbled upward as stones filled the room where it was chained, only to die of suffocation when it reached the end of its leash. A group of priests had abandoned their last meal of fish and eggs to flee the tremors; some were struck down when a portico collapsed on top of them, while most of the others were asphyxiated in a building where they sought shelter. One determined individual, however, had tried to fight his way out; he used an axe to cut his way successively through the building's partition walls, only to meet his fate when he came up against an impenetrable barrier of lava. In their poignant immediacy, the Pompeiian casts provide a unique snapshot of death in action, fixed for the centuries in a mould of lava.

Life before disaster

As Pompeii and Herculaneum re-emerge from the lava that encased them for so long they are revealing more of their secrets every day. The edifices of many other ancient cities were gradually dismantled for building stone, or the settlements were slowly modified by later communities until the older towns were virtually unrecognizable. In contrast, much of the architecture of Pompeii and Herculaneum is remarkably intact – even the roofs of some of the buildings have survived. Archaeologists have been able to study private homes, from luxurious mansions to houses divided into several apartments in which poor families often shared one room. Among the buildings that have been excavated are shops, public baths, and even a brothel, its walls decorated with erotic frescoes. In addition to the buildings, the thousands of objects still being rescued from the rubble include statues, metal tools, jewelry and papyrus scrolls.

This wealth of material has provided invaluable insights into the daily lives and beliefs of the inhabitants of the two ill-fated cities. The temples testify to the importance of the official state religion, which honoured the Olympian gods and deified emperors. Religion was also a private affair – images of special household deities, called *lararia*, have been found in shrines in many homes. Some citizens clearly appreciated poetry and music and no doubt attended performances at the towns' two theatres. However, the best-attended public events must have been the wild-beast fights and gladiatorial games that were held in Pompeii's great amphitheatre. (On the day of the eruption, 60 gladiators died in their barracks there.) Traces have even been found of civic life at the moment of the disaster; 79CE was an election year, and political slogans and graffiti still cover many of the walls. Yet not everyone would have been entitled to vote in the election that never happened, because this was a slave society – most of the bodies found in Pompeii are in fact those of slaves, identified by the broad belts that signified their wearer's lowly status.

right: Many of Pompeii's inhabitants appear to have belonged to mystery cults. This detail from a fresco in the House of Mysteries, which was sacred to the Dionysian cult, depicts the god Pan and the female Panisk; to the right stands a terrified, veiled woman.

NORTHERN SHIP BURIALS

In the ninth and tenth centuries CE, people across much of northern Europe lived in fear of attacks by Vikings, the seagoing warrior-traders of Scandinavia. Accounts of their terrifying raids were recorded in monks' chronicles along with details of their pagan practices and of their shallow-draughted longships, which could be rowed up rivers as well as sailing the seas. More than a thousand years after the onslaught began, the discovery of a buried Viking ship filled with grave goods was to allow scholars to paint a dramatic picture of the lifestyle of a Norse chieftain.

In April 1880 the sons of a farmer living near Gokstad on Norway's Oslo Fjord decided to investigate a tumulus, traditionally known as the King's Mound, that rose on the family's land. Word of their intentions reached Nikolas

Nikolyasen, president of the Oslo Antiquarian Society, who hurried to the site to ensure that appropriate archaeological techniques were employed. It took just two days of digging for his team to uncover the prow of a magnificent wooden ship. For the next two months, his men laboured to clear the thick blue clay that covered the vessel. They prevented the newly-exposed oak timbers from drying out by dousing them regularly in water and covering them with spruce boughs.

The Gokstad ship

Once it had been cleaned up and restored, the Gokstad vessel turned out to be a masterpiece of the Viking ship-builder's art. Constructed in the late ninth century CE, it was more than 75 feet (23 m) long and would have held a crew of around 70 men. There were 16 oar ports on each flank, and 64 wooden shields still decorated its sides.

Nikolyasen was disappointed to find that grave-robbers had penetrated the mound hundreds of years earlier, removing the richest grave goods. However, the ship still housed furnishings that vividly evoked a Viking chief-tain's life: half a dozen beds, most of which were easy to dismantle so that they could be taken on expeditions; an iron cauldron big enough to contain food for 50 men; and even a box full of games, including a draughts-board.

Better still, the remains of the ship's owner were found. To judge from the skeleton, he was a strapping man, at least 50 years old who had stood more than 5 feet, 10 inches (1.8 m) tall. The bones also revealed that he had been afflicted by gout, a finding that led some scholars to speculate about his identity. He might, they suggested, have been King Olaf Geirstada-Alf, a semi-legendary king of southern Norway in the ninth century CE, who

left: A picture stone carved in Ardre in Gotland, now a Swedish island in the Baltic Sea. The complex composition on the stone includes a Viking ship (centre left) with a crew of warriors. Such vessels were often burned or buried along with their dead owners.

The Oseberg Ship

The remains of another magnificent Viking-age vessel were found 24 years after the discovery of the Gokstad ship, just 9 miles (15 km) away in southern Norway. Similarly preserved by a blanket of blue clay, the Oseberg vessel (see illustration, below) was more beautifully decorated than its companion, with wood carvings of exceptional quality, but it was also markedly less seaworthy. Tree-ring dating has suggested a possible reason; built as early as 820CE, at a time when sails were first being introduced in Scandinavia, the ship may have been constructed to an experimental design. It is in fact the earliest-known Viking sailing vessel.

The ship contained an extraordinary collection of artefacts, from household furnishings and looms to a full-sized cart and four sledges. Together, they would have catered for all the afterlife needs of its two female occupants: a woman aged about 50 and another of 30.

Given the magnificence of the burial, the older woman was almost certainly a queen – possibly Asa, grandmother of Harald Fairhair, who would one day unite Norway. The younger woman was probably a servant, sacrificed to accompany her mistress into the afterlife.

Like the Gokstad ship, the Oseberg boat had been attacked by tomb robbers, who had treated its royal occupant with scant respect. The queen's skeleton was missing a right hand, the fingers of the left hand and the upper left arm, all apparently cut off for the rings and bracelets that they bore.

was known to have suffered from the condition. Around the body lay the bones of sacrificial animals: 12 horses, six dogs and, surprisingly, a peacock.

above: This gold, garnet and glass decoration is all that survives of a purse lid, probably made of whale-bone ivory, that was found at Sutton Hoo. The purse itself was a leather pouch containing gold coins. It would have been attached to a wide leather belt using the three hinges at the top and fastened with the catch at the bottom.

Boats for the dead

Ship-settings, as the Scandinavians call such burials, have a long history. More than 400 have been excavated from all over Scandinavia and Britain, and that figure probably represents only a small proportion of the total. Norse custom placed the body in the boat, which was expected to carry the deceased on a journey to the afterlife.

Yet the ship-settings were by no means limited to the Viking era. On the Swedish island of Gotland, which is particularly rich in them, they date back deep into the Bronze Age, to about 1000BCE. Another impressive cache comes from the Vendel region, on the mainland north of Stockholm. These boat graves, crammed with rich funerary goods including helmets decorated with plates of moulded bronze, double-edged swords with inlaid hilts and pommels, and luxury foreign ornaments, have given their name to a whole era of

Swedish history, the Vendel period, stretching from approximately 500 to 800CE.

Besides the corpses actually interred in boats, there was also a Scandinavian tradition of burials within ship-shaped graves, marked out with standing stones arranged in the familiar longship design, with higher stones at the prow and stern. Such customs, along with the tradition of burning boats and bodies, indicate that the ships in ship burials were regarded as symbolic rather than as actual vessels ferrying the dead on their final voyage.

Other cultures also linked boats and the afterlife. In the 1990s, archaeologists at Abydos in Egypt dug up a fleet of more than a dozen vessels, each between 65 and 100 feet (20 and 30 m) long, which had been buried as part of the funeral rites of a 1st-dynasty pharaoh 5,000 years ago. In the Egyptian tradition, however, the ships were set alongside the deceased's tomb as grave goods. The logic seems to have been rather different to that of the Viking burials, in which the ship represented the soul's journey to another world. The Egyptians more likely had in mind the sun's nocturnal journey by boat through the underworld.

Sutton Hoo

One of the most celebrated ship burials was discovered not in Scandinavia but in England. In 1939 at Sutton Hoo archaeologists investigated a series of mounds overlooking the Deben River near the Suffolk coast. The largest turned out to contain the remains of a ship that was 100 feet (30 m) long. Although the planking had rotted away, the impression left by the timbers was preserved, along with the metal rivets that had held it together. The craft was mastless and had evidently been propelled by oars.

> "His boon companions carried their beloved chief to the seashore, as he had commanded when he still had a voice. Rime-crusted and ready to sail, a royal vessel with curved prow stood at hand. They laid their dear king amidships, hard by the mast. A trove of treasure had been foregathered from far afield. No ship, some say, was ever so well stocked with swords and corselets, weapons and armour ... "

(THE FUNERAL RITES OF THE LEGENDARY DANISH KING SCYLD SCEFING, AS DESCRIBED IN BEOWULF, OLD ENGLISH EPIC CA. 700–750CE)

There were many surprising aspects to the Sutton Hoo find. One was its location, for ship burials were only known from Scandinavia at the time. Another was the fact that the mound contained no body, nor any indication that there had been one. However, residual traces of phosphate have since been found, suggesting that a corpse might once have lain there, only to rot away completely in the acidic conditions created as the ship's planks decayed.

Who was the individual who had been so honoured in death? The grave goods, which included a fearsome helmet and weapons, indicated that he was male and a warrior, and their magnificence suggested that he was a person of considerable power and wealth, almost certainly a king. England was divided at the time into a number of different realms, one of them East Anglia where the body was found. East Anglia's rulers are known to have had a palace at Rendlesham, just 3.5 miles (6 km) from where the mound stands.

There were other clues to the king's identity in the accompanying grave goods. Coins left in a decorated purse (see illustration, opposite) indicated that he had probably died between 600 and 625CE. The geographical reach of the trove, including silverware from distant Byzantium and weapons from Sweden, suggested that he had wide international contacts. More intriguingly, there were hints in the mound of Christian influences, even though the very concept of ship burial was intrinsically pagan; a spoon that bore the names Saul and Paul – those of Saint Paul before and after his conversion – looked suspiciously like a Christening gift.

Historical records in fact suggested a likely candidate: Raedwald, one of the few East Anglian kings to have exerted wide sway outside his own dominion. He had died ca. 625, fitting the dates assigned by the coins. In addition, a reference in Bede's *Ecclesiastical History of the English Nation*, the best source for the period, suggested an explanation for the religious confusion displayed in the mound. Raedwald, Bede wrote, " … had been admitted to the Christian faith in Kent, but in vain; for on his return home, he was seduced by his wife and certain perverse advisers, and turned back from the sincerity of the faith [to paganism] … so that, like the ancient Samaritans, he seemed at the same time to serve Christ and the gods whom he had served before".

The finds at Sutton Hoo fit that description perfectly, and they also indicate why no further burial mounds were found. Within a couple of years of Raedwald's death, his successors definitively abandoned the old gods for the Christian faith. The gradual spread of Christianity would eventually put an end to the custom of ship burial across the entire northern world. However, that process was a slow one; 300 years after the raising of the Sutton Hoo monument, ship burials were still being practised in other parts of Europe.

The burial rites

In the year 922CE the Arab writer and diplomat Ibn Fadlan travelled up the Volga River on a deputation from the Caliph of Baghdad. There he met the Vikings known as Rus, a name these warrior-merchants would one day pass on to the land of Russia in which they traded. In the river port of Bulgar Ibn Fadlan witnessed the funeral of one of their chiefs. The lengthy description he left is the most detailed account of a Norse ship burial to have come down to modern times.

Ibn Fadlan reported that for 10 days before the obsequies the man's body lay in a temporary grave while the necessary arrangements were made. His worldly goods were split three ways, one part going to his daughters and wives, another on mortuary garments to clothe the corpse, and the third to provide *nabid* – a strong alcoholic drink – for the mourners. His family sought a volunteer from among his slave girls to accompany him into the afterlife. When one came forward, she was held to her word and was not allowed to change her mind.

In the interval before the last rites took place, the dead man's companions brought his longship ashore and set it on a timber frame amid what Ibn Fadlan called "large wooden figures in the semblance of human beings" – presumably statues of Norse gods. Seamstresses prepared the dead man's funeral outfit, which included a gold-trimmed kaftan and a hat of gold damask and sable. Meanwhile, the chosen slave girl was decked out in finery and encouraged to enjoy herself.

When the appointed day finally came, the corpse was taken from its temporary resting place, where the cold had kept it relatively unspoiled, although the skin had blackened. Dressed up in its new clothes, it was carried to the ship and propped up on a splendidly-decked couch inside a tent amid all the trappings of a banquet. The dead man's weapons were placed around him. Meanwhile, animals were sacrificed: a dog was hacked in two, and a pair of horses were driven until they were in a lather and then cut to pieces, which were thrown onto the ship. Two cows were also killed, and a rooster and a hen were decapitated.

The slave girl was then taken to a wooden structure resembling a door-frame. The men accompanying her

"You take the people who are most dear to you and whom you honour most and put them into the ground where insects and worms devour them. We burn him in a moment, so that he enters Paradise at once."

(A "RUS" INTERPRETER TO THE ARAB WRITER IBN FADLAN AT THE SCENE OF A NORSE SHIP BURIAL IN 922CE)

lifted her up to peer above it three times. On each occasion she uttered words that Ibn Fadlan did not understand. When he asked for a translation, he was told that she was looking into the afterlife; the first time she said she could see her father and mother, the second time her dead relatives, and the third time her master, who was calling her to join him in paradise.

She was then taken to the ship, where an old crone known as "the Angel of Death" was waiting for her; Ibn

left: This iron helmet from the Sutton Hoo ship burial was shattered when the burial chamber collapsed and has been carefully restored. The helmet has panels of tinned bronze decorated with animal motifs and heroic scenes. Each eyebrow culminates in a gilt-bronze boar's head, symbolizing strength and courage.

the ribs with a broad-bladed knife while the men strangled her. Male attendants outside beat their shields with their staves in order to create enough noise to drown out her screams, which, according to Ibn Fadlan, "might have terrified the other girls, and deterred them from seeking death with their masters in the future".

Leaving the girl dead behind them, the killers clambered down from the ship, and a stark naked man approached it bearing a blazing torch. This was the dead man's next of kin, come to ignite the firewood stacked under the frame. Others followed with additional fire-sticks. Soon the pyre was fully ablaze, consuming the chief, the girl and all the assembled grave goods. Meanwhile, Ibn Fadlan added, a storm had blown up that only served to stoke the flames.

This extraordinary account of a terrible and awe-inspiring series of events is of course an outsider's view. No doubt a Viking would have told the story differently. There is no reason, however, to doubt its general accuracy, maybe even heightened by the objectivity of the observer. It is worth repeating at length because it suggests vividly the potent mixture of naked power, religious exaltation, physical intoxication and sheer terror that must have lain behind many of the sacrificial rituals described in this book, sanitized as they otherwise are by the passage of centuries. In none of these respects were the northern cultures unique – virtually all the different elements of human sacrifice displayed have their equivalents across all five continents.

Fadlan described her as a dark, thick-set woman with a grim countenance. The girl was given *nabid* to drink that apparently so befuddled her that she could not find her way into the tent, at which point the old woman unceremoniously dragged her in by the hair. Six men then laid the girl down by her master's side, where she was held by the hands and feet. The old woman looped a rope around her neck, giving the ends to two of the men to pull. She herself repeatedly stabbed the girl in

THE QILAKITSOQ CORPSES

On 9 October 1972, two brothers, Hans and Jokum Grønvold, were on a hunting expedition to the abandoned settlement of Qilakitsoq on Greenland's west coast when Hans suddenly stumbled upon two undisturbed graves.

The remoteness of the site, about 280 miles (450 km) above the Arctic Circle, meant that archaeologists did not investigate the burials until 1977. Between them, the two graves were then found to contain eight naturally mummified bodies, stacked one on top of another. The first grave to be opened held three women, ranging in age from the early 20s to the mid 40s; above them lay the corpse of a four-year-old boy and, uppermost, a six-month-old baby. The second grave accommodated three women, two of them about 50 years of age and the third one, in the middle, probably in her late teens.

The bodies had been desiccated by the cold, dry air. The position of the graves had also helped to preserve the corpses. Located under a natural rock overhang, they were protected from direct sunlight and rain.

Studying the mummies

The contents of the graves were examined at Denmark's National Museum. Four of the bodies were eventually returned to Greenland, and are now on display in the Greenland National Museum in Nuuk. Carbon-14 dating of sealskins also found in the graves revealed that the burials dated back to about 1475 CE. The dead were found to be from the Thule culture; their people had arrived from northern Canada in about 1000 CE, and were the ancestors of today's Greenland Inuit.

"I started to poke around and realized that I had found a grave which had never been opened before. ... There was a half-grown child lying on top, close to what was probably its mother, and then we saw a doll which had fallen to the side, a doll which turned out to be a little child ... "

(HANS GRØNVOLD, REPORTING THE DISCOVERY OF THE QILAKITSOQ BODIES IN A LETTER TO A FRIEND)

The scientists sought to establish the family relationship of the dead people by matching up tissue types. This evidence suggested that the oldest women in each of the two graves might have been sisters, a probability strengthened by the fact that they wore almost identical facial tattoos.

Another line of enquiry concerned the reasons why the bodies were buried together. The idea that the various individuals might all have drowned in a single boating accident was soon abandoned. No traces of sand were found in their clothes, and there were no signs of diatoms or other tiny sea creatures in their tissues.

Starvation was also ruled out as a cause of death, as most of the bodies showed adequate levels of subcutaneous fat. There were no symptoms of tuberculosis or any infectious diseases, nor any signs of recent injuries. The only conclusion that the researchers could draw was that the eight people probably died separately of various causes, and were buried at different times rather than in a single mass interment.

Signs of ill health

However, a couple of the bodies did bear evidence of serious ill health that might have been life-threatening. The four-year-old had a misshapen pelvis indicative of Down's syndrome. In the harsh conditions of fifteenth-century Greenland, such children were

left: This baby was the best preserved of all the Qilakitsoq dead because, being the smallest, it had lost its body heat quickest and therefore had suffered the least from the processes of decomposition.

in order to soften it for clothing. Their lungs were blackened with soot from the blubber lamps used to light the turf-and-stone huts in which they lived, causing the condition known as "black lung".

Inuit style

The greatest surprise of the find was the clothing. The women wore the heavy sealskin trousers, anoraks and *kamik*s (thigh-length boots stuffed with insulating grass) that continued to be normal wear for the Greenland Inuit into recent times. The restored garments exhibited a remarkable sense of style, employing sophisticated patterning and combinations of light- and dark-coloured skins that would not look out of place in a modern-day boutique. To judge from what they wore, the fifteenth-century Greenlanders were far more than subsistence hunters – such elegant tastes could hardly have been expected in people facing the harsh conditions in which they lived.

The care taken in dressing the corpses also says much about enduring Inuit beliefs about the afterlife. The soul, as well as the body, was thought to benefit from warm clothing, which would serve it in the next world, conceived as very similar to the one it had just left.

sometimes left to die of exposure, and it is possible that such was the young boy's fate.

Yet the condition of one of the older women showed that adults able to fend for themselves could survive even in the face of severe physical handicaps. She had suffered malnutrition as a child. More significantly, she bore the marks of a cancer that had eaten its way from the nasal passage to her left eye, leaving her deaf and partially blind. Even though the cancer no doubt caused the woman's death, the evidence of her fingernails showed that she had continued to work until her final days, scraping and preparing sealskins.

In other respects, the scientists' verdict on the women's health was no less gloomy. Their teeth were grooved due to years of tearing animal sinew to make thread, and were worn down from chewing sealskin

chapter 4

THE NEAR EAST AND GREECE

From Civilization's Dawn

THE JERICHO SKULLS

THE DEATH PITS OF UR

EAST OF EDEN

DEATH IN CRETE

HOMER'S HEROES

THE MACEDONIAN MONARCH

MOUNTAINTOP MAUSOLEUM

THE JERICHO SKULLS

If Africa was the birthplace of the human race, the Middle East was its first breadbasket. The transition from hunting and gathering to a more settled agricultural way of life was almost certainly the most radical change to occur in prehistory, with huge implications for human health, culture and religion. This major change first got under way in the area known as the Fertile Crescent – the horseshoe-shaped sweep of land stretching around the Arabian Desert, from the Zagros Mountains of Iran through northern Iraq, Syria and southern Turkey to Lebanon and Israel. Such a revolution could hardly but have affected people's attitudes toward death. A series of extraordinary portrait skulls, found first in the Jordan Valley and subsequently at other sites around the Crescent, suggests the forms those changes took.

Strange skeletons

The first skulls were excavated by the English archaeologist Kathleen Kenyon at Jericho from 1953 on. She dug into a tell, or mound, near the modern city, cutting through the layers associated with biblical times and on down to the first signs of human habitation. The site turned out to have been inhabited as early as 9000BCE, on the cusp of the farming revolution. Kenyon traced its development over the next 1,700 years, as it gradually grew from a hamlet, occupied by settled hunter-gatherers who experimentally planted wild strains of wheat, into a large village of scattered, circular houses, surrounded by a solid stone wall and overlooked by a massive watchtower. Then, from about 7300BCE on, the architecture changed again. The buildings became straight-walled and multi-roomed. The old, haphazard living conditions were giving way to the regularity dictated by incipient town planning.

It was over the next millennium that the skulls were produced. At the time bodies were buried under the floors of houses, or in the spaces between dwellings. Intriguingly, Kenyon found that most of the skeletons, at least of adults, were headless. At some point the skulls had been detached and buried separately in skull pits.

Some skulls, however, were preserved for special treatment. The faces were coated with plaster and modelled with noses and ears, apparently to create a portrait of the dead individual. Shells took the place of eyes. Often the jaw was missing, perhaps because it had become separated as the body decayed, but in a few cases the entire head was preserved. The backs of the skulls

left: Discovered at the Jericho archaeological dig, this plaster-coated human skull with shell eyes dates from the 7th millennium BCE. The bands of brown paint across the forehead may represent a headdress, which could signify the individual's social status.

The Jerusalem Tombs

Fascinating light was cast on a much later period in the Holy Land's history by the discovery in 1968 of a Jewish cemetery just to the northeast of Jerusalem. Workmen building new housing stumbled on a complex of caverns containing burials from the early Common Era. One of the ossuaries contained an inscription in Aramaic, the language of Israel in New Testament times, that identified one occupant as "Simon, builder of the Temple" – a reference to King Herod's temple, built some time after 20 BCE.

More evocatively still, another ossuary contained the remains of a man who had been crucified – a relatively common punishment in the Roman era. He was identified as "Yehohanan, son of Hagakol", and medical examination indicated that he had been between 24 and 28 years of age and had stood 5 feet, 6 inches (1.68 m) tall. The evidence of his suffering was graphic: one of the heelbones was still pierced by the thick iron nail that had been used to attach him to the cross.

above: *Jerusalem's Kidron Valley contains many tombs. Some date back to the 8th century BCE but most are from the Second Temple period ending in the 1st century CE.*

usually remained unplastered, suggesting that the finished models were intended to be viewed from the front.

Remembering the dead

Kenyon herself believed that the skulls were the product of some sort of ancestor cult, and there seems little reason to quarrel with her view. The heads were apparently designed to be displayed as reverential, if macabre, memorials to the town's notable dead. Unless further spectacular discoveries are made, there is no way of knowing just who was singled out for this special treatment – civic dignitaries, priests, cherished relatives – although nearly all the skulls were those of adult males.

What is evident, though, is that such behaviour was a relatively new development. The nomadic life of hunter-gatherers had allowed little scope for commemorating the dead, given that there were limits to the number of momentoes that they could carry around. Their grief at the death of loved ones was no doubt just as acute as that of their successors, but in practice they had few opportunities for memorializing those who passed on. A cult of the dead, as evinced by the Jericho skulls, requires a more settled lifestyle, as well as somewhere to exhibit the preserved remains.

Jericho is still the earliest walled town known to archaeologists. The skulls found there show that its builders had crossed another important threshold in their attitude to death – henceforth, the past could live on in a way that it never could in the unending present of the hunter-gatherer lifestyle.

THE DEATH PITS OF UR

If ever a past civilization can truly be said to have been rescued from oblivion, it is that of ancient Sumer. The world's earliest cities flourished there, the wheel and plough were put to use, and writing was invented. Yet for more than two millennia this hothouse of innovation, where the seeds of learning and culture germinated and urban life began, lay buried under desert sands.

Sumer was the earliest of the civilizations of ancient Mesopotamia, a region in what is now southern Iraq whose name in Greek means "the land between rivers", namely the Tigris and Euphrates. Mesopotamia itself suffered much the same fate as Sumer, remembered in latter times mainly through passages in the works of Greek historians such as Herodotus and Xenophon and from hostile references in the Bible to Babylonian captivity and Assyrian conquest. Mesopotamia's glory was eventually eclipsed, first by the Persians and then the Greek conqueror Alexander and his successors. When the region rose to prominence again in the eighth century CE, it was under Islamic rule, notably in the person of Haroun al-Rashid, the caliph of *Arabian Nights'* fame. For all their love of learning and the arts, he and his Muslim successors had little interest in the pagan cultures that had predated the Arab conquest. Over the ensuing centuries, the remaining traces of Mesopotamia's former splendour gradually disappeared.

The discovery of cuneiform
The first steps in Mesopotamia's rehabilitation were taken by Western

below: A Sumerian weight, made of hard diorite and shaped like a duck, bears an inscription in "cuneiform" script. The term was coined by scholars in the 17th century CE from the Latin *cuneus*, meaning "wedge".

scholars. As early as the seventeenth century, an Italian traveller, Pietro della Valle, had brought back tablets inscribed with strange, wedge-shaped markings. The deciphering of the language, which was dubbed "cuneiform", was a lengthy business that had to wait on the discovery of additional material for scholars to construe. The hunt was to prove both long and dangerous. A Danish expedition sent to the Near East in 1761 under the leadership of Carsten Niebuhr brought back vital inscriptions from Babylon, but the other five of its six members died of disease on the way. In the 1830s the English scholar-adventurer Sir Henry Rawlinson (see page 112) copied

turned out to form an almost complete version of the Epic of Gilgamesh, the world's oldest literary work. We now know that the epic – the most famous passage of which describes its hero's quest to find the secret of immortality – originated in Sumer and was based on a historical ruler of Uruk, who lived sometime after 2750BCE.

The Akkadian mystery

As scholars familiarized themselves with the language of the Assyrian tablets, they found that it was the same tongue that had been used by the Babylonians. Scholars dubbed this language Akkadian, from the earlier state of Akkad, whose ruler

As Akkadian became better understood, however, it also appeared even more mysterious. It seemed to belong to the Semitic family, with similarities to such later tongues as Hebrew and Arabic. Yet the cuneiform script it was written in was poorly adapted to Semitic speech patterns – for example, Akkadian lacked a means of conveying the variable vowel sounds that are a feature of all Semitic languages. Gradually the view spread that the Akkadians must have adopted the script from an earlier, non-Semitic people who had spoken a different tongue. It was the French scholar Jules Oppert who first gave them a name. Noting the formula "King of Sumer and Akkad" that appeared in some early inscriptions, he suggested in 1869 that the creators of cuneiform, and so of the art of writing itself, must have been Sumerians.

> "When the gods created humankind, they appointed death as the lot of humans, keeping eternal life in their own hands."
>
> (FROM THE EPIC OF GILGAMESH)

---

one crucial trilingual inscription while standing on a ladder balanced on a ledge barely 1 foot, 6 inches (0.5 m) wide that lay 330 feet (100 m) up a sheer cliff-face.

A vital breakthrough came in 1849, when the English archaeologist Austen Henry Layard uncovered the library of the Assyrian king Assurbanipal in his ancient capital of Nineveh. Layard and his team recovered more than 24,000 cuneiform tablets. Some of these

Sargon had built an empire in the area south of Babylon in the twenty-fourth century BCE. Although Akkadian proved to be a difficult tongue to decipher, steady progress was made. In 1857, Britain's Royal Asiatic Society sent a copy of a newly-discovered inscription independently to three leading experts, including Rawlinson. When this work was completed, the respective translations were found to tally in all essential details.

In search of the Sumerians

At first the people Oppert had named remained shadowy and insubstantial, but subsequent scholarship verified his extraordinary piece of linguistic detective work. Even so, visible evidence of Sumerian civilization was still lacking on the ground. That too, however, began to change as the nineteenth century progressed. Between 1877 and 1900 Ernest de Sarzec, a French diplomat in the Persian Gulf port of Basra, excavated a series of mounds at Telloh, located in the desert of what is now southern Iraq. There he found the remains of the Sumerian city of Girsu. Among his many discoveries was a series of sculptures, carved in the hard rock called diorite, that turned out to be more than 4,000 years old.

Before Sarzec, an Englishman named J.E. Taylor had done some preliminary work on a site near the Euphrates that was to prove even more significant than Telloh/Girsu

in Sumerian history. By coincidence, it was the same mound from which della Valle had rescued the first cuneiform inscriptions to reach the West more than 200 years before. Although Taylor lacked the means to conduct a full-scale excavation, in 1854 he tunnelled into the remains of what had been a ziggurat, or stepped temple, and discovered

inscribed cylinder seals buried in its foundations. From the inscriptions, Henry Rawlinson was able to identify the site as the city of Ur – familiar to readers of the Old Testament as Ur of the Chaldees, the birthplace of the biblical patriarch Abraham.

Because of its biblical connections, Ur was a name to conjure with, and its rediscovery was to be

crucially important to the resurrection of Sumer at the fountainhead of history. However, some time was to pass before Ur was properly explored. In the intervening years, other sites turned up crucial finds, all tending to confirm the extent and splendour of the lost civilization: an American team from the University of Pennsylvania dug up the remains of the city of Nippur, while the German Robert Koldewey excavated sites near Telloh. It was only after the First World War, when Iraq fell temporarily into British control under a League of Nations mandate, that funds were found to mount a full-scale expedition to Ur, under the direction of the British archaeologist Leonard Woolley.

Uncovering Ur

Woolley was 42 years old when he started work at Ur in 1922. He had studied at Oxford, and had been Assistant Keeper of the university's famous Ashmolean Museum. He had already worked at Carchemish in Syria and in the Sinai desert before being sent to Ur under the joint sponsorship of the University of Pennsylvania and the British Museum.

At first Woolley focused much of his attention on a subsidiary mound 2.5 miles (4 km) from Ur. The site, known as Tell al-Ubaid, had already been excavated three years previously by another English archaeologist, H.R. Hall, who had dug up quantities of distinctive pottery there. This Ubaid ware would eventually be found across much of southern Mesopotamia and beyond, giving its name to the entire historical period immediately predating the foundation of the early Sumerian dynasties. Woolley continued Hall's work, showing the mound to have once been an inhabited island rising out of the marshes that covered the surrounding area in ancient times.

Woolley's discoveries at Ur itself were on an altogether grander scale. In all, his workers dug through strata representing five millennia of occupation, ca. 5500–500BCE. The site was then abandoned, presumably because the Euphrates, which had once linked it to the Persian Gulf, had changed its course, leaving it landlocked. Today, it stands 6 miles (10 km) away from the river, surrounded by desert wastes.

In 1927 Woolley turned his attention to an area on the edge of the city that he had already tentatively identified as a burial ground. In fact he found two separate cemeteries. It was in the older one that he made his most spectacular discoveries. In all, it contained 660 separate graves. The vast majority belonged to ordinary citizens, most of whom were either wrapped in reed matting for burial or else placed in a coffin of clay or wood. Some were buried with jewelry, mirrors, weapons and other personal possessions, and bowls and jars containing foodstuffs were also found in many of the pits, apparently left there by mourners. Woolley took these grave offerings as evidence of belief in an afterlife in which the dead person would have need of such goods.

left: The ruined walls of Ur overlooked by its stepped temple platform, or ziggurat, ca. 2100BCE, dedicated to the moon god Nanna. The ziggurat was first excavated by Leonard Woolley's team in 1923.

below: An ornate sheath and a gold-bladed dagger, with a handle decorated with gold studs and lapis lazuli, found in Queen Puabi's tomb in the royal cemetery at Ur.

The royal tombs

The real excitement of the cemetery lay in its oldest part, where Woolley found 16 much more elaborate burials. In these the bodies were laid to rest in specially-constructed stone chambers, capped by vaulted or domed roofs. Each one was situated at the bottom of a sizeable rectangular pit, typically 33 feet (10 m) by 16 feet (5 m) across and as much as 28 feet (8.5 m) deep; access was down earthen ramps. Woolley dubbed these sites the "royal tombs", and the discovery of two incised cylinder seals bearing the names of kings gave credence to the title. Most of the royal tombs at Ur have since been dated to ca. 2600BCE.

Almost all the royal tombs had been despoiled by grave robbers, evidently in ancient times, but a couple survived intact. One contained the body of a woman whom an accompanying seal identified as Queen Puabi, her skull still adorned with a spectacular headdress of golden leaves, flowers and rings. Other grave goods found here and elsewhere included golden bowls, daggers and helmets, as well as remarkable figures fashioned from gold and lapis lazuli, a treasured gemstone that had to be imported to Ur from distant sources in eastern Iran.

Dying for the king

For all the treasures found with the bodies, however, the most striking feature of the burials was the manner in which the rulers had been laid to rest. The floors of the pits outside the tombs were littered with the bodies of dead people and animals. In one case, no fewer than 74 corpses were found; 68 of them were women, all elaborately robed in scarlet and each accompanied by a lyre. Another tomb was guarded by the bodies of six soldiers, each of whom had worn a copper helmet and carried a spear. With them were the remains of two wagons and the six animals that had drawn them, along with three other human corpses – possibly those of the wagons' drivers and an accompanying groom.

To Woolley the significance of such scenes was plain – these were attendants who had gone willingly to their death with their royal masters in a demonstration of voluntary human sacrifice on an almost unparalleled scale. Cups found with most of the bodies even suggested how they might have died: by drinking poison, or else drugs that left them unconscious. "Then," Woolley wrote, "someone came down and killed the animals and perhaps arranged the drugged bodies, and when that was done earth was flung from above onto them, and the filling in of the grave shaft was begun."

As Woolley imagined the scene, the pit was closed in stages; as each layer of earth was added, further sacrifices were made, and libations and other offerings were presented to the underworld gods. Once ground level had been reached, some kind of funerary chapel was built to mark the spot. In Woolley's view, it was the presence of these mortuary buildings that in later years attracted commoners to the site to bury their dead, until in time it became a cemetery for the entire community.

Recently Woolley's interpretation has been challenged, partly in the light of forensic evidence suggesting that all the attendants did not die at precisely the same time. Scholars have proposed an alternative scenario, in which deceased courtiers who had been associated in their lives with the dead monarch might have been exhumed from temporary graves and reinterred at the time of the royal funeral.

However, such an explanation raises problems of its own. In particular, it does not sit easily with the mixture of human and animal remains found in the death pits, unless some combination of fresh animal sacrifice and human reinterment was involved. In the absence of any firm literary evidence describing the nature of funeral rites in early Sumerian times, any reading of what exactly happened there 4,500 years ago must remain provisional. For the time being at least, Woolley's vision of rulers departing for the afterlife to the sound of harp and lyre in the company of gaily-dressed and willing associates seems to fit the known facts as well as any alternative suggestion.

Uncovering an Ancient Crime

When Woolley's labourers excavated the resting-place of Queen Puabi in 1927, they also discovered an adjacent tomb pit that overlapped that of the queen. In this second tomb they found the remains of 25 bodies, six of them male and 19 female. Its unidentified occupant too was evidently royal, and Woolley surmised from the positioning that he had been Puabi's husband. Almost all the grave goods had been stolen in antiquity, and Woolley was even able to suggest who the culprits were. A hole had been dug between the two tombs, presumably by the workmen who excavated Puabi's burial place sometime after the death of her consort. Knowing the riches that lay in the adjoining vault, they had evidently broken in and removed them. To conceal the opening they had made, the thieves used a wooden chest – it remained there undisturbed for 4,500 years.

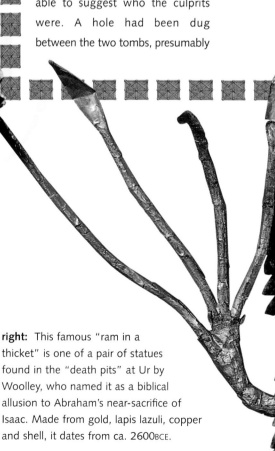

right: This famous "ram in a thicket" is one of a pair of statues found in the "death pits" at Ur by Woolley, who named it as a biblical allusion to Abraham's near-sacrifice of Isaac. Made from gold, lapis lazuli, copper and shell, it dates from ca. 2600BCE.

EAST OF EDEN

The world's largest prehistoric cemetery lies not among the tumuli of Brittany or the barrows around Stonehenge, but on an island in the Persian Gulf. Excavations of some of the thousands of burial mounds there have cast new light on an enduring archaeological mystery – the identity of Dilmun, a fabled eastern land of plenty. Folk memories of Dilmun may even have contributed to the biblical account of the Garden of Eden.

For all its historic importance, Dilmun's very name was lost for millennia, along with knowledge of the Sumerian language in which it was preserved. That changed when the forgotten tongues were deciphered by the British adventurer-scholar Henry Rawlinson and others in the nineteenth century CE (see pages 106–111). Texts uncovered at various Mesopotamian sites, including the library of the Assyrian king Assurbanipal at Nineveh, were found to describe Dilmun as an earthly paradise, blessed by the god Enki with abundant crops, flocks and precious metals.

An idyllic island?
Further evidence of Dilmun's mythic significance came from its association with the Epic of Gilgamesh (see page 107). A version of the tale found late in the nineteenth century in the ruins of the Sumerian city of Nippur revealed where the hero's search for immortality took him: to "the land of Dilmun, the place where the sun rises".

Other ancient texts portrayed Dilmun as a land where sickness and savage beasts were unknown and water gushed unsought from the ground to irrigate the fields. Just as elements of the Flood story, also contained in the Epic of Gilgamesh, found their way into the biblical account of Noah, so fragments of these tales may have influenced the Old

"In Dilmun the raven does not croak ...
the lion does not kill
nor the wolf slaughter the lamb ...
The invalid does not say 'I am ill',
The old do not complain 'I am aged'."

(LINES FROM A TABLET FOUND AT NIPPUR, SINGING THE PRAISES OF DILMUN)

Testament vision of Eden as a paradise garden in the east. Such reports might have been taken for the stuff of legend, but inscriptions found elsewhere in Mesopotamia indicated that Dilmun had been a real place. Specifically, a text dating to the reign of Sargon of Akkad (see page 107) made "ships from Dilmun tie up at the quays" of his capital, Agade. Dilmun had evidently not merely existed, but had harboured a maritime trade.

It was Rawlinson who, in an act of inspired historical guesswork, first suggested the location of Dilmun: Bahrain, in the Persian Gulf. The island has indeed always been unusually fertile, and for a reason that makes the link with Enki entirely understandable. The god's domain was the *apsu*, a freshwater ocean believed to lie far beneath the Earth, while Bahrain in fact owes

right: Dilmun was perfectly located on the trading routes between Mesopotamia and the Indus Valley. Carved stamp seals such as these, ca. 1200BCE, recall Dilmun's trade relations with the world outside.

its fecundity to a subterranean aquifer that supplies the island's abundant artesian wells.

The burial fields

Most of the speculation about Dilmun remained purely literary until the 1950s, when a Danish team of excavators set out to explore Bahrain's archaeological heritage. One of the expedition leaders, Geoffrey Bibby, described in his book *Looking for Dilmun* how at first sight the sheer number of tumuli took his breath away: "As far as the eye could see to either side, a sweep of 10 miles (16 km) or more, there was no end to the mound field; there must have been tens of thousands of mounds on view."

On excavation, most of the mounds were found to contain a central stone chamber barely large enough to hold a body, ringed by a low wall. Typically, each contained a single corpse, with the body laid on its right side and the head sometimes protruding into a specially-provided alcove. Most have been dated to the period from 2100 to 1700BCE, when Dilmun's prosperity was at its peak.

Examination of the corpses, which were of all ages and both sexes, provided tantalizing glimpses of the lives of Dilmun's citizens. Average life expectancy was just short of 40. The dead were buried with pottery and sometimes joints of meat, suggesting that they expected to need sustenance for a post-death journey. Dental examinations showed that they suffered from a high incidence of tooth decay, perhaps through eating the sweet dates for which Bahrain has long been famous. By modern standards their lifestyle was less than paradisiac, but in the context of their own time they were indeed probably among the world's more privileged citizens.

below: The ancient honeycombed burial complex at Sar is one of many in Bahrain – there are tens of thousands of graves in different locations, with a number of types of mound identifiable.

DEATH IN CRETE

In 1979, Greek archaeologists working on the island of Crete made an extraordinary discovery. Yiannis and Evi Sakellarakis were investigating a hillside site named Anemospilia – the Cave of the Winds – close to the small town of Archanes and about 4.5 miles (7 km) from the island's ancient capital, Knossos. There they found a small, rectangular building dating back to the middle of the Minoan period – the era some 3,700 years ago when Crete boasted one of the early world's most sophisticated civilizations. Scholars had long thought of the Minoans as being a largely peace-loving people. Yet inside the building at Anemospilia the Sakellarakises found startling evidence that seemed to confirm the practice of human sacrifice in Minoan Crete. Their discovery is still causing controversy among historians to this day.

The building consisted of three unconnected rooms giving off a linking passageway. The only furnishings found were fixed stone benches in the east and west rooms, along with a clay platform in the central one. There were, however, clues as to what the building's function had been. A monumental pair of limestone horns had once adorned its facade, linking the structure to the bull cult commemorated in the Greek legend of Theseus and the Minotaur (see box, opposite). More bizarrely, a pair of life-sized clay feet were found on the bench in the central room; they had apparently once supported a

below: A bull-jumping fresco from the palace at Knossos, ca. 1500BCE. Bull motifs were common in Minoan times, when the beasts were apparently venerated for their strength and virility.

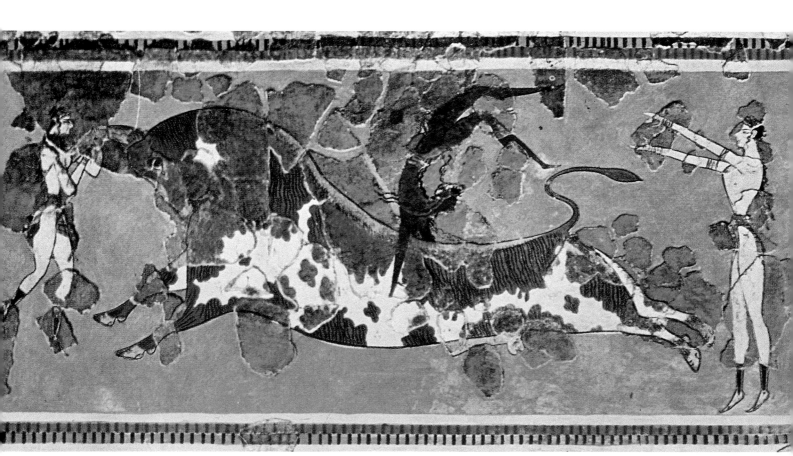

wooden statue that had been destroyed in ancient times along with the building itself. The location of the statue, and the large number of votive pottery shards found in the east room, indicated to the excavators that the structure had been a small temple. The central statue had evidently represented the god who was worshipped there.

Sacrificed in vain

The discoveries in the west room were far more macabre. It contained the remains of three bodies – two men and a woman. Forensic examination revealed that the woman was in her late 20s and the elder man in his late 30s. But the investigators focused most attention on the third body – that of a young man about 18 years old – which was found lying on the stepped bench. One leg was bent up awkwardly at the knee, suggesting that it might have been trussed in place with ropes; the position of the body resembled that of a trussed sacrificial bull depicted on a Minoan vase found elsewhere. More strikingly still, a large bronze blade decorated with a boar's head rested where the boy's abdomen had been.

The Sakellarakises came to the conclusion that the young man had most likely been a sacrificial victim. As if to confirm the suspicion, the badly burned remains of a fourth body were found in the corridor, surrounded by fragments of a bucket-shaped vase decorated with the image of a bull. Just such a container is known from other sources to have been used in Minoan Crete to collect the blood of sacrificial animals.

Further evidence for the theory came with the dating of the remains. The temple was destroyed ca. 1700BCE, at the time when the royal palace at Knossos and other important buildings also collapsed. A clear scenario now seemed to open up. Alarmed by foreshocks of a disaster that was to devastate all Minoan Crete, the keepers of the shrine had sought to placate the gods by offering up a human sacrifice. Yet the act was to no avail. They could barely have drained the boy's blood into the sacrificial vessel when a massive earthquake struck. The devastation of the shrine was completed by fires probably started by the torches used to light it.

Theseus and the Minotaur

Scholars have long linked Crete's bull cult with the celebrated Greek myth of Theseus. This story harked back to a time when the people of Athens were compelled to send seven youths and seven maidens every ninth year to the court of King Minos. On arrival, the 14 youngsters were dispatched to an invariably fatal encounter with the Minotaur, a monster with the body of a man and the head of a bull. Volunteering to rid the world of this horror, Theseus travelled to the island and ventured into the maze-like Labyrinth, designed by Daedalus, in which the monster lived. Theseus succeeded not only in killing the beast – by using a concealed sword – but also found his way back to safety with the help of a ball of twine unravelled by Ariadne. Mythographers think that the story may have been inspired by travellers' accounts of the genuinely labyrinthine layout of the palace of Knossos and of the remarkable bull-jumping feats that took place there.

Such an interpretation of the events at Anemospilia has not gone unchallenged. Dennis Hughes, in his 1991 book *Human Sacrifice in Ancient Greece*, has cast doubt on every element of it, suggesting that the building may not have been a shrine, the blade might have fallen onto the boy's body from above, and his leg may have been accidentally curled up, since his hands were not bound. Yet the sequence of events described by the Sakellarakises has a ring of plausibility. If their reading is indeed correct, the finds at Anemospilia not only provide unique evidence of human sacrifice in ancient Crete but, even more strikingly, give eloquent testimony of a sacrifice that failed.

HOMER'S HEROES

The story of how a self-made, self-educated German businessman set out to discover the lost world of Homeric Greece is one of the great epics of archaeology. In the late nineteenth century CE Heinrich Schliemann determined to devote his boundless energy and considerable fortune to proving that the world the father of Greek poetry had portrayed in the *Iliad* had really existed. Schliemann believed the tale it told of a nine-year siege of Troy by a confederation of Greek rulers, culminating in the fall and destruction of the city.

The Homeric account implied that the siege had taken place around 1250BCE. Classical-era Greeks accepted it as a historical reality, and saw it as the high point of a lost heroic age. However, the only evidence to support this view was the ancient poetry, passed down orally, that Homer had drawn on. With the passing of classical Greece, even knowledge of the site of Troy was lost. It was known to have lain somewhere on the Turkish coast near the mouth of the Bosphorus, but that was all.

Schliemann's quest

Schliemann's first concern was with finding Troy. There were two possible contenders – both substantial mounds. One lay outside a village called Bunarbashi, about 5 miles (8 km) inland from the Aegean near the Bosphorus's southern mouth. The other site, Hissarlik, was only 3 miles (5 km) from the sea. Schliemann preferred the claim of Hissarlik, for Homer had described the Greek warriors as moving rapidly from their boats to Troy. Also, the poet had pictured Achilles pursuing the Trojan Hector three times around the city walls; yet when Schliemann set out to run around the mound at Bunarbashi, he found that a steep crevice blocked the way.

At the time most scholars regarded Schliemann's blind faith in the accuracy of Homer as foolish, for the poet had lived almost 500 years after the events he purported to describe. Yet Schliemann's trust in the *Iliad* paid off. As soon as he started digging at Hissarlik, in 1870, he found traces of massive walls. The following year his

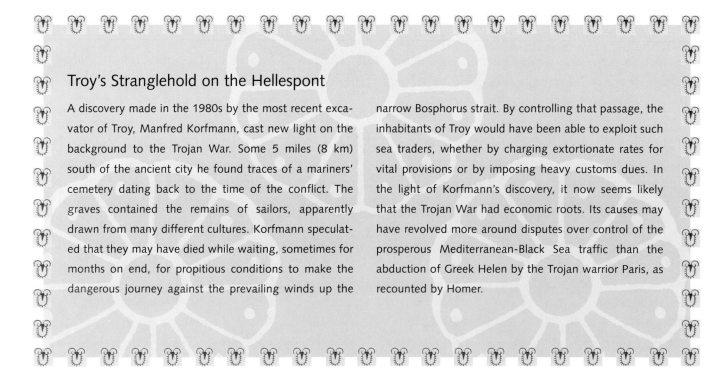

Troy's Stranglehold on the Hellespont

A discovery made in the 1980s by the most recent excavator of Troy, Manfred Korfmann, cast new light on the background to the Trojan War. Some 5 miles (8 km) south of the ancient city he found traces of a mariners' cemetery dating back to the time of the conflict. The graves contained the remains of sailors, apparently drawn from many different cultures. Korfmann speculated that they may have died while waiting, sometimes for months on end, for propitious conditions to make the dangerous journey against the prevailing winds up the narrow Bosphorus strait. By controlling that passage, the inhabitants of Troy would have been able to exploit such sea traders, whether by charging extortionate rates for vital provisions or by imposing heavy customs dues. In the light of Korfmann's discovery, it now seems likely that the Trojan War had economic roots. Its causes may have revolved more around disputes over control of the prosperous Mediterranean-Black Sea traffic than the abduction of Greek Helen by the Trojan warrior Paris, as recounted by Homer.

above: Archaeologists now believe that there have been nine settlements at Troy, covering a period of more than 3,000 years. This cult sanctuary forms part of the remains of Troy 7, the Greek-era town built ca. 1200–1180BCE, just after the Trojan War.

workers cut a deep trench through the mound, which stood 165 feet (50 m) high. What they found was not one but many ancient cities: layer upon layer of occupation stretching back over hundreds or even thousands of years.

The "Treasure of Priam"

The real payoff for Schliemann's work at Troy came in 1872, when he uncovered an extraordinary treasure of golden vessels, weaponry and jewelry. Schliemann at once dubbed the trove the "Treasure of Priam", the city's legendary ruler, and insisted that it had been found in a building he had already identified as Priam's palace. The truth was in fact more complicated. According to an assistant on the site at the time, the scene of the discovery was actually a tomb outside the building.

In addition, the gold was found at a level that, as subsequent investigation showed, long predated the Homeric city. In all, Schliemann himself identified seven

different levels of occupation, a number that later researchers increased to nine. The first five dated back to the early Bronze Age, between about 3000 and 1900BCE; the next two – Troy 6 and 7 – came closer to the traditional dating for the siege, covering the years ca. 1900–1100BCE. The last two layers were clearly post-Homeric: Troy 8 was built ca. 700BCE (following a gap of some 400 years when the site was unoccupied), and was inhabited by Greeks; Troy 9 endured into Roman times.

Priam's Treasure, which was found in Troy 2, is now thought to have been more than 1,000 years older than Priam, dating back to ca. 2500BCE. Who it was made for remains a mystery, for Troy's occupants were illiterate until the seventh century BCE. The trove, however, indicates that there was great wealth in the city at that early time.

The search for the besieged city

The walls of Troy 6 had something of the massive quality that Homer's descriptions suggested, if on a smaller scale. Yet attempts to identify this city, which thrived ca. 1900–1300BCE, with the Homeric one foundered on a stubborn fact: convincing archaeological evidence indicated that it was destroyed by an earthquake, not military action.

To complicate matters further, Level 7, which approximated with the siege's traditional dating, showed three separate periods of disruption over about 200 years. The first, 7A, was the only one that bore unambiguous evidence of military assault, including the contorted skeletons of bodies left to lie where they fell; as a result, it is the one that scholars now generally associate with the fall of Troy. The other two episodes left no such obvious signs of fighting, although there was evidence that the city burned down in the final catastrophe that brought Level 7 to an end. However, that event happened around the year 1100BCE – too late for the chronology traditionally assigned to the siege.

The Troy Schliemann laid bare fell considerably short of the mighty citadel evoked by the Homeric epic. It was a well-defended city, strategically placed on an important trade route leading from the Mediterranean to the Black Sea; and the discovery of the treasure indicated that at times in its history it must have known great wealth. Its streets – to judge from the evidence of Level 6 – were paved with massive stone blocks, and its citizens used implements of bronze and employed pottery brought by trade from the far side of the Aegean. Yet its size was unimpressive by modern standards: the fortified area was no more than 650 feet (200 m) across. Its cramped

"I have gazed on the face of Agamemnon."

(HEINRICH SCHLIEMANN, ANNOUNCING THE DISCOVERY OF THE GOLDEN FACE MASK AT MYCENAE)

confines can hardly have provided room to house the "topless towers of Ilium" that Homer's words evoked.

Mycenae's secrets

Schliemann subsequently turned his attention to the other side of the Aegean. After Troy itself, no location in the *Iliad* had greater resonance than Mycenae. This was the home of Agamemnon, the leader of the Greek confederation. It was also the place where, on his return from the nine-year siege, he was butchered by his wife Clytemnestra and her lover, as recounted in the other great Homeric epic, the *Odyssey*. This was the man whose tracks Schliemann now determined to follow.

There was at least no problem about identifying the site of Mycenae, fragments of whose massive walls had survived from classical times. The English Lord Elgin had already investigated the ruins. But Schliemann, remembering Homer's epithet "Mycenae rich in gold", was convinced that more remained to be discovered. He was particularly interested in the tomb of Agamemnon, described by the second-century CE Greek traveller Pausanias as lying within Mycenae's walls.

Most nineteenth-century scholars insisted that Pausanias must have been referring to some long-lost city walls, not the massive ramparts of the citadel that had survived to their day. They had good reason

left: This gold diadem, ca. 1500BCE, was found in one of the shaft graves at Mycenae. Such objects suggest that the city's ruling families enjoyed great personal wealth and could afford to indulge in expensive burials.

above: The gold face mask Schliemann found at Mycenae has proved controversial. Certainly redolent of a hero, it almost certainly belonged not to Agamemnon, but to an earlier member of Mycenae's ruling family.

for so arguing, for the citadel sat atop a steep knoll, enclosing a small area of mostly bare rock that seemed highly unsuitable for burials. Moreover, empty burial places were plain for all to see lower down in the valley below Mycenae. Called "beehive tombs" from the shape of their domed interiors, these huge, monumental structures were clearly built to receive royal or noble dead.

The face of Agamemnon?

Once again, however, Schliemann confounded the experts. High up in the citadel, behind its famous Lion Gate, he found evidence of burials that descended directly into the rock, in some cases as deep as 15 feet (4.5 m). In these shaft graves, Schliemann again struck gold. In all, half a dozen graves were found, containing the remains of 19 men, women and children, all of them adorned with the precious metal and surrounded by a trove of grave goods that easily surpassed even Priam's Treasure. In the last of them, the excavators found a well-preserved corpse bearing a golden facemask depicting the visage of a bearded warrior. This man, Schliemann decided, must have been Agamemnon himself.

Schliemann in fact had again underestimated the age of the objects that he had found. Current opinion dates the shaft graves to between 1600 and 1450BCE, at least 200 years before Agamemnon's time. In discovering them, Schliemann had travelled back even beyond the Trojan War era to unearth relics of the Mycenean civilization's early days in the Bronze Age centuries of the second millennium BCE.

THE MACEDONIAN MONARCH

Athens and Sparta may have been the chief centres of Greece's classical age, but by the fourth century BCE a new power was in the ascendant – Macedon, on the nation's northern border. The king who steered Macedon to glory from 360 to 336BCE was Philip II, father of

above: This marble bust from the Vergina royal tomb bears a strong resemblance to surviving portraits of Philip II of Macedon and was long used as evidence to support the case for identifying the tomb's human remains as belonging to the great king.

the future Alexander the Great, who would carry Macedonian arms to the limits of the known world.

Archaeologists long speculated about the whereabouts of Philip's tomb, which was known to lie at a place ancient sources called Aigai, located where the Thessalonian Plain rose up to the mountains of the Greek peninsula. One frequently considered candidate was the village of Vergina. In a region where ancient burial mounds are relatively common, Vergina had the biggest of all – the Great Tumulus, 360 feet (110 m) in diameter and still 40 feet (12 m) high.

Vergina's royal tombs

The Great Tumulus was excavated from the 1950s on, but the break-through only came in 1977 when the Greek archaeologist Manolis Andronicos uncovered three tombs. One was empty but for magnificent wall-paintings of the rape of Persephone by the underworld god Pluto; tomb robbers had evidently looted the contents in antiquity. A second tomb was intact, and contained rich grave goods in gold and silver, as well as the cremated bones of a young man.

However, it was the third tomb that became the focus of interest. The tomb consisted of two small rooms, a burial chamber and an antechamber. It too was unlooted, and the burial goods were particularly

rich. Most significantly, each room contained a marble sarcophagus containing a small gold chest decorated with the sunburst motif of the Macedonian royal house. And in each casket were the cremated bones of a dead person, wrapped in purple cloth woven with golden thread.

The body in the antechamber turned out to be that of a woman between 25 and 27 years old. The occupant of the main room had been a man. The cremation had not been thorough; in place of ashes whole bones had survived, charred and slightly warped by the flames. Putting them together, the investigators found they had the almost-complete skeleton of an individual between 35 and 55 years of age who had stood 5 feet, 6 inches to 5 feet, 8 inches (1.67–1.72 m) tall. The tomb was fairly obviously royal, and the fittings dated it to the second half of the fourth century BCE. Could these be the remains of Philip II?

Manolis Andronicos certainly thought so, and there seemed to be compelling evidence to support his view. Besides the regal integuments, he noted that one of the grave goods bore the unusual name "Machatas", known to have been that of one of Philip's brothers-in-law.

Andronicos' judgment appeared to be confirmed when a team of British researchers studied the charred remains found in the tomb. They came to the conclusion that the dead man had suffered a traumatic injury – a wound to the face that had left him blind in the right eye. And Philip himself had indeed lost an eye, 18 years before his death, when he was struck by an arrow fired from the walls of a city he was besieging.

Father or son?

Recently, however, other forensic scientists have challenged this conclusion. Where the British team saw evidence of an arrow wound, they see only natural grooving of the bone; in addition, they could find no sign of the regrowth of bone fabric that would inevitably have occurred as the body sought to heal itself. The new investigators put down other distortions in the skull not to physical injury but to the effects of cremation.

Other scholars had earlier questioned the identification of the body as Philip's on points of dating. The tomb was barrel-vaulted, a technique thought to have reached Greece from the orient only after the eastward odyssey of Philip's son Alexander. Certain of the tomb goods also suggested a date at the end of the century, too late for Philip II. As a result, a rival name was put forward for the corpse: Philip III Arrhidaeus,

right: This gold casket contained the cremated remains of the occupant of Vergina's controversial royal tomb.

Alexander's stepbrother and eventual heir as ruler of Macedon, who died in 317BCE.

The recent forensic evidence would seem to tip the balance of probability in favour of the son rather than the father – Philip III, not Philip II – although arguments for and against will no doubt continue to reverberate. What is not in doubt is that the find

remains a major breakthrough, bringing modern archaeologists into contact with Alexander the Great's closest relatives. And, appropriately for a survivor of Greece's heroic age, the dead ruler had been sent to the grave in true Homeric fashion: cremated on a funeral pyre, with his remains set in a golden container buried deep under a huge memorial mound.

"Then they laid [Patroclus's bones] in a casket of gold and wrapped it around with a robe of purple; presently they put it away in the hollow grave, and piled over it huge stones packed closely together."

(THE BURIAL OF PATROCLUS AS DESCRIBED IN HOMER'S *ILIAD*. THE MACEDONIANS APPARENTLY FOLLOWED IDENTICAL RITES FOR THE INDIVIDUAL BURIED IN THE VERGINA MOUND.)

MOUNTAINTOP MAUSOLEUM

On a remote mountaintop in eastern Turkey lie the eerie ruins of a remarkable mausoleum. A manmade tumulus at the summit is accessed via three stepped terraces, where the remains of giant stone sculptures of gods and ancient rulers gaze out over the plain below. Built on a grand scale, the mausoleum represents a bid by its creator to carve out a kind of immortality for himself.

In ancient times, Anatolia – now the Asian part of Turkey – was an extraordinary meeting ground of peoples, serving as a bridge between East and West. Here the Hittite, Phrygian and Lydian cultures flourished, along with outposts of Greek civilization on the Aegean coast.

The influence of Greece spread further across the plateau in the wake of Alexander the Great, who swept through Anatolia on his way to defeat Persia in 334BCE. After his death, Anatolia fell under the rule of one of his generals, Seleucus, and his successors. However, from 200BCE on Seleucid control was challenged by the rising power of Rome. Local rulers took advantage of the prevailing uncertainty to establish personal fiefdoms. One such was the small kingdom of Commagene, sandwiched between Cappadocia and Cilicia in what is now eastern Turkey. Commagene flourished for nearly 200 years thanks to its position on a major east–west trade route.

"So I planned this monument as a foundation secure from the ravages of time near [the gods'] heavenly thrones. In it my body, having endured blessedly through to old age, will sleep for eternity, once my soul, loved by the gods, has gone forth to Zeus Oromasdes' heavenly throne."

(Antiochus I's inscription describing his goal in building the terraces at Nemrut Dag)

Antiochus I's dream

Commagene won its independence at some point in the second century BCE, and came to serve as a buffer state between the rival empires of Rome and Parthia. It might have passed as a forgotten footnote into the history books had it not been for the overweening ambition of one ruler, Antiochus I. In the mid-first century BCE this king decided to commemorate his reign by building a unique mountaintop mausoleum – a *hierothesion*, or "dwelling place of all the gods next to the heavenly thrones" – to receive his body.

He chose to site the monument on what he called the "topmost ridge" of his kingdom, so his remains should be as close as possible to the gods, and he planned its construction on a massive scale. The amount of labour involved must have been staggering, for he decided to level three separate terraces at the top of a 7,200-foot (2,200-m) peak, one of the highest in the Anti-Taurus range. The debris from the clearance was piled up on the summit to create a tumulus 164 feet (50 m) high. Beneath it, the king's body is thought to lie in an as-yet undiscovered tomb.

One of the terraces was left bare, but for a statue of an eagle and a wall of standing slabs. The other two were lined with colossal stone sculptures of Antiochus's antecedents and of the gods they worshipped, some of them as much as 33 feet (10 m) high. Because of Commagene's position at a crossroads of cultures, both ancestors and deities were a heterogeneous bunch. On his father's side, Antiochus traced his ancestry to the Achaemenid rulers of Persia, while the matrilineal line was Greek, stretching back to Alexander the Great. The divinities too were a mix of Greek and Persian: Zeus was identified with Ahura Mazda, and Apollo with Mithra, the Persian god of light.

The death of a dynasty

The empty terrace may have been designed to receive the remains of Antiochus's successors for centuries to come, but if so the king's hopes were to be disappointed. Soon after his death, his kingdom became a Roman province and his dynasty came to an end. The mausoleum mouldered unvisited on its lofty eyrie, and was forgotten by all but local people. Westerners only became aware of its existence in the late nineteenth century, when German travellers came across the spectacular ruins. One Turkish and one German report were subsequently prepared. Further investigation was delayed until the 1950s, when a team led by American archaeologist Theresa Goell carried out extensive researches.

Today the monument is known by its Turkish name of Nemrut Dag – literally Mount Nimrod, the name of the peak on which it lies. Earthquakes and erosion have taken their toll on the statuary, toppling gods and rulers and leaving rows of seated torsos facing out over a surrealistic jumble of shattered stonework and huge, detached heads. In many ways the chaos seems to mock Antiochus's ambitions to broadcast his fame. Yet, perversely, he is remembered today for the monument he created, while the name of the kingdom that he ruled has all but been forgotten.

left: A massive stone head of a god or ruler atop the summit of Nemrut Dag surveys the land around – for eternity.

chapter 5

EAST ASIA AND THE PACIFIC

FIRST STIRRINGS IN ASIA

THE TARIM BASIN MYSTERY

THE PAZYRYK NOMADS

CHINA'S IMPERIAL TOMBS

KEYHOLE TOMBS OF JAPAN

ENIGMATIC EASTER ISLAND

Emperors and Explorers

FIRST STIRRINGS IN ASIA

In 1891 a Dutch anatomist by the name of Eugène Dubois made discoveries on a Javanese riverbank that were to prove vital for the study of human ancestry. What he found were fossil remains: a couple of teeth, the top of a skull, the thighbone of a primate that had evidently walked on two legs. Dubois himself believed that he had found evidence of the "missing link" between apes and man posited by the theory of evolution, which Charles Darwin had proposed just three decades before (see page 10). Dubois duly christened his find *Pithecanthropus erectus* – literally "upright apeman".

Since its discovery, however, Java Man, as the finds became known, has been reassigned by paleontologists. The remains are now recognized as belonging to a species also known from Africa: *Homo erectus*, the first fully human being (see page 12). Other, similar fossils – around 40 in all – have also been discovered on the island, amounting to about a third of all the *Homo erectus* finds worldwide. They have also turned out to be even older than Dubois could have imagined: a recent dating suggested that two of the fossils were as much as 1.74 million years old.

The China mystery

Even earlier human remains have been found in China, where a tooth and a fragment of a jawbone found in Longgupo Cave have been dated back as far as 1.78–1.96 million years. China was also home to the famous Peking Man fossils, discovered in the Zhoukoudian caves near the capital Beijing in the 1920s and 1930s (see box, right). These bones too were assigned to *Homo erectus* and were dated as being around 460,000 years old, indicating that early humans may have survived in East Asia for 1.5 million years.

below: Rice paddies stretch out near the lower Yangtze River. Early inhabitants of China would have had to survive without this famous staple, which was only cultivated from ca. 4000BCE on, relying instead on hunting and gathering.

The Zhoukoudian site also shows evidence of much later phases of occupation. The so-called Upper Cave was inhabited as recently as 10,000 years ago, but by a different species: *Homo sapiens*, or anatomically modern humans (see pages 11–12). The unsolved mystery of Asian prehistory revolves around the huge gap between this date and the earlier ones, and the question of genetic continuity. Did the *Homo sapiens* population, which we know was present all across East Asia by 10,000 years ago, evolve out of the earlier *Homo erectus* communities? Or did *Homo erectus* die out, to be replaced by a second wave of immigration from Africa, where both *Homo erectus* and *Homo sapiens* probably originated, more than a million years later? Was Asia peopled not once but twice?

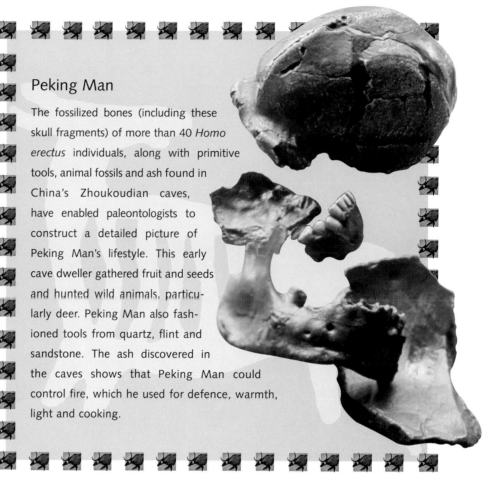

Peking Man

The fossilized bones (including these skull fragments) of more than 40 *Homo erectus* individuals, along with primitive tools, animal fossils and ash found in China's Zhoukoudian caves, have enabled paleontologists to construct a detailed picture of Peking Man's lifestyle. This early cave dweller gathered fruit and seeds and hunted wild animals, particularly deer. Peking Man also fashioned tools from quartz, flint and sandstone. The ash discovered in the caves shows that Peking Man could control fire, which he used for defence, warmth, light and cooking.

Journey to a new land

The current evidence allows no firm answers to these questions. However, the latter hypothesis was lent considerable weight in summer 2003 when news emerged from Africa of the discovery of a 160,000-year-old skull classified as a subspecies – *Homo sapiens idaltu* – of modern-day humans, which it is theorized emigrated from Africa and replaced the remnants of the first, pre-human diaspora. Whether there were two waves or one, the journey across Asia must have been a daunting one. It would have been made by small hunter-gatherer bands maybe 20 to 30 people strong. The migrants would have had to cope with winters in which the temperature fell as low as -40°C, and with biting winds blowing across treeless steppe. To survive such conditions, *Homo erectus* would almost certainly have needed fire; the colonization of the cold lands of Eurasia is in fact the most convincing argument suggesting that this crucial skill was acquired at an early date. The payoff for all the hardship would have come in fine hunting opportunities, for the wide plains were grazed by herds of reindeer, bison, horses and mammoth.

Homo sapiens groups are thought to have made their way eastward primarily along the fringes of a band of woodland that stretched from southern Europe to the South China Sea. Reaching the virtually impassable tropical forest that covered much of southern China, they then swung either northward toward northern China and the Zhoukoudian region or southward into Southeast Asia. An alternative route crossed the grasslands of what is now Kazakstan into Siberia. That direction led to the frozen north – but also eventually on to the Bering Strait land bridge and America (see pages 38–9).

THE TARIM BASIN MYSTERY

The Tarim Basin lies in what is now China's westernmost province of Xinjiang, to the north of Tibet. Much of its hot, dry expanse is taken up by the Taklamakan Desert, the second largest in the entire Eurasian landmass. In ancient times, however, the region played an important role at the heart of the Silk Road trade route, linking China and the West. In recent decades hundreds of desiccated bodies, many 2,000–4,000 years old, have been found in the area. The first discoveries were made early in the twentieth century by European explorers. Most, however, have been exhumed since the late 1970s by Chinese and local Uighur archaeologists.

Intriguingly, the majority of the bodies look surprisingly Western in appearance, showing Caucasoid facial features that are more typical of Europe than of the Orient. Of 300 skulls examined so far only 11 percent are considered to have the Mongoloid characteristics generally associated with the population of China and eastern Asia – an odd fact that raises the question of what the ethnic origin of the others might have been. For the most

below: The Taklamakan Desert, seen here, has preserved the Tarim Basin bodies in good condition. The land on the desert's fringes attracted settlers because it had water and lay astride the Silk Road.

part, these remarkable Bronze Age corpses have fair skin, reddish-blond hair and long noses – traits not shared by any of the ethnic groups inhabiting the region today.

Archaeologists in the provincial capital of Urumqi are now struggling, with the help of scholars from the USA and Europe, to unravel the many mysteries of the Tarim Basin corpses. What were these Western-looking people doing so far east at such an early date? How long were they there for? Where had they come from? And what caused their eventual disappearance from a region where they had evidently lived for well over 1,000 years?

To compound the puzzle, the clothes found on some of the Tarim corpses show close similarities with other fabrics found at Hallstatt, a famous Bronze Age site far away in the Austrian Alps. Some of the Tarim Basin mummies' clothes even display tartan patterns, suggesting a link with the Celtic cultures of western Europe. Preliminary results from DNA testing have also supported the idea of a connection with Western peoples.

Qarqan Man

One of the most striking finds was made at Zaghunluq, a site close to the town of Qarqan (also known as Cherchen) in the southeastern Tarim. The remains were those of a man about 55 years old who died approximately 3,000 years ago (see illustration, page 130). His body now lies, alongside others that are almost equally well preserved, in a museum in Urumqi.

Qarqan Man's corpse arouses many emotions in the viewer. One is a feeling of repose – at first glance it is quite easy to think he is sleeping. Another immediate response is surprise at just how un-Oriental he looks; the long brown hair, plaited into twin braids, appears distinctly Western, as does the wispy brown beard, and even the sheer size of the body. In life, the man must have stood a full 6 feet, 6 inches (2 m) tall.

On closer inspection, there are oddities about the corpse that are hard to explain. There is a design painted in yellow ochre across the face, but what its significance might have been is impossible to say for sure. Pigment was found with the body in the grave, suggesting that

the face-painting may have formed part of a funerary ritual. Some scholars have professed to see a link between a sun symbol painted on the man's temple and Mithraism, a Persian solar cult that spread widely in Roman times. Equally intriguing are the clothes buried with the body. Qarqan Man wore trousers – a recent invention in his day, for the fashion seems to have come in with horse-riding, which had originated on the steppes not long before (see page 132). Certainly he himself could ride, for a leather saddle was buried with him. The skull and front leg of a horse were interred close by.

Natural mummification

There are also questions about the remarkable state of preservation of Qarqan Man's corpse. As with the

The Beauty of Loulan

The earliest preserved corpses yet discovered in the region come not from Zaghunluq or the other southern oases but from Loulan at the basin's eastern end, close to the Chinese nuclear testing site of Lop Nur. One body in particular caught the imagination of the Uighur people. The remains were those of a woman who had been about 5 feet (1.5 m) tall, her long brown hair framing a face that conveyed a great sense of tranquillity even in death. Carbon dating subsequently indicated that she had died around 1800BCE, which means that she was an approximate contemporary of the biblical Abraham. The archaeologist who discovered her named her the "Beauty of Loulan", and the label stuck. When the body was put on display, local people saluted her as "the mother of the Uighur nation", and popular songs were even written in her honour.

other Tarim Basin bodies, this was largely due to the peculiarities of the Taklamakan Desert in which they lived and died.

In earlier ages the basin was a shallow inland sea that eventually dried up, leaving vast salt deposits scattered about its bed. As a result, the desert soil is not only sandy but also salty, providing ideal conditions for preserving fleshy tissue. In that respect, the desert's natural salts performed much the same function as the artificially applied natron of the Egyptian mummifiers. Bodies buried in the desert in winter were effectively freeze-dried by the combination of the cold, dry climate and the salty earth. The Tarim people clearly had some understanding of this process; archaeologists have found several corpses that had been deliberately buried in a way that allowed air to circulate around the extremities, thus aiding desiccation.

Aridity, salinity and the extreme cold of winter were enough to protect the earliest Tarim corpses, but it is possible that by the time of Qarqan Man's death nature was being helped out by more direct human intervention. Chinese scientists who examined the corpse soon after its discovery reported that it was coated with a yellow dust. Laboratory tests subsequently suggested that the substance involved was some form of animal protein, but nothing else could be ascertained.

Tocharian origins?

The greatest enigma, however, remains the Tarim corpses' ethnic origins, and here manuscripts written in an otherwise unknown Indo-European language provide a further twist to the mystery. These ancient texts, also from the Tarim Basin oases, caused a considerable stir when they first showed up in British India in the 1890s, supplied through local middlemen; indeed, they were what first drew the attention of Europeans to the Tarim

left: The body of Qarqan Man was found in the same grave as three women and a three-month-old baby; all are thought to have been killed by an epidemic. In addition to his bright clothing, Qarqan Man was buried with 10 hats, each of a different style.

region. The language was dubbed Tocharian, after a central Asian people known to classical authors as the Tochari. Bizarrely, Tocharian proved on analysis to be grammatically closer to such Western languages as Latin and Greek than to geographically nearer branches of the Indo-European tree such as the Slavic or Indo-Iranian tongues. The Tocharian manuscripts came mainly from the eastern end of the Tarim Basin, where most of the Caucasoid mummies have also been found.

In ancient times, the area played a pivotal role at the heart of the Silk Road and the likelihood of a link between the mummies and the manuscripts is seemingly strengthened by paintings found in Buddhist cave shrines along the famous trade route. These show apparently Western-looking individuals with deep-set eyes, light hair and beards, suggesting that the mummy people's genetic inheritance might have survived down many generations. Even so, some scholars are cautious about identifying the mummies as Tocharian because of a yawning time gap: most of the manuscripts date from about 500–700CE, and the cave paintings from ca. 900CE, more than two millennia after the older corpses were interred.

The long journey eastward

The solution to the mystery of the mummies evidently lies buried in the early history of the Tarim Basin region, and unfortunately much of that remains obscure. However, archaeologists have turned up evidence of a Bronze Age farming culture, the Qawrighul (named for a cemetery site near Lop Nur), whose people lived in villages growing crops and raising animals. Some were also skilled craftsmen, and their artefacts show an affinity with the Afanasevo culture of southern Siberia to the north. The greatest change to affect the Qawrighul people's peaceful lives – there are no weapons in their graves – came with the introduction of horses, sometime around 1000BCE. Horsemanship opened up the mountain grasslands on the basin's edges, turning the farmers into seasonal pastoralists, moving their flocks between the high valleys in summer and the desert edges in winter.

"That moment as I held her in my arms and looked at her lovely face, I knew she was the most beautiful woman I had ever seen. I knew that if she had been alive today, or if I had been alive 3,000 years ago ... I would most certainly have made her my wife."

(ARCHAEOLOGIST HE DEXIU DESCRIBING HIS EMOTIONS ON DISCOVERING THE BODY OF A 1,500 YEAR OLD WOMAN AT ZAGHUNLUQ IN 1989)

The Afanasevo connection is probably the best clue to the Tarim people's origins. The Afanasevans are generally thought to have formed part of a largescale movement of Caucasoid peoples eastward from the region between the Volga River and the Ural Mountains that got under way at some point around the mid-fourth millennium BCE. They themselves settled down in the area of Siberia north of the Tarim, occupying lands in the Altai Mountain foothills southwest of the modern city of Krasnoyarsk. It seems likely that an offshoot of this group may have found their way through the mountains, arriving in the Tarim Basin around the year 2000BCE. There they lived quietly and apparently contentedly for more than two thousand years, until a rising tide of Chinese immigration gradually overtook them in the course of the first millennium CE.

The Tocharians, if that is what they are rightly called, were never forcibly dispossessed of their lands. Rather, they seem to have interbred with the incomers, slowly losing their separate identity. Their genetic inheritance lives on in the local population – even now, it is not unusual to see red-haired individuals in the streets of Urumqi. It may be wrong, then, to call the Tarim Basin Caucasoids a lost people. In reality, they may never have gone away at all.

THE PAZYRYK NOMADS

Around the year 450BCE Herodotus, ancient Greece's celebrated "Father of History", visited an area north of the Black Sea in what is now the Ukraine. There he encountered the Scythians, the name the Greeks gave to the tribes of nomadic horsemen who lived in the region. Herodotus's Scythians

below: A late Scythian mummy skull with a funeral mask made of plaster, which has been painted in an attempt to preserve the deceased's features.

in fact formed only a small part of a great multitude of peoples, all of them sharing similar, horse-based lifestyles, who inhabited the vast sweep of steppeland stretching uninterrupted from modern Romania in the west to Mongolia and the borders of China in the east. These peoples were the very first to ride horses, sometime around 1000BCE.

Herodotus gathered all the information that he could about these wandering tribesmen, reporting that they lived in tents (which resembled the yurts of modern Mongolian herders) and spent the year travelling in search of pasture for their herds of sheep, cattle and horses. He noted the Scythians' fearsome

reputation as warriors; they beheaded dead enemies, scraping the scalps clean for use as napkins and transforming the skulls into leather-bound drinking cups.

Mourning a Scythian king

The Scythians' elaborate burial rites particularly fascinated Herodotus. He described in detail the 40-day period of mourning that marked the death of a king. The royal corpse was mummified, he wrote – the innards were removed and sweet-smelling spices were inserted in the cavities – and covered in wax. The preserved body was then paraded around the king's former dominions. At each stop, the menfolk cropped their hair and lacerated

"They take the king's corpse and, having opened the belly and cleaned out the inside, fill it with a preparation of chopped cypress, frankincense, parsley seed and aniseed, after which they sew up the opening, enclose the body in wax and, placing it on a wagon, carry it through all the different tribes."

(THE GREEK HISTORIAN HERODOTUS, DESCRIBING SCYTHIAN ROYAL BURIAL CUSTOMS CA. 450BCE)

themselves, cutting their ears, noses, foreheads and arms; in addition, each man was expected to stab an arrow through his left hand in token of his mourning.

Once it had completed this posthumous progress, the royal body was taken to a remote part of the steppe and laid in a square grave, set on a mattress in a roofed space covered with timber thatching. Grave goods, including magnificent Greek goldware, were placed around the corpse, along with the bodies of sacrificial victims, both human and animal. Meanwhile, the chief mourners took part in purification rites that included the use of narcotics; inside a small tent they threw hemp seeds onto red-hot stones and inhaled the smoke, which, according to Herodotus, made them "noisily exultant".

An even more elaborate rite took place a year later, on the anniversary of the monarch's death. At that time, Herodotus claimed, 50 of the king's attendants were strangled and mummified, along with 50 of his horses. The horses were then arranged in a circle around the royal tomb, each one with its belly supported on a stake so that it seemed to be still standing. The 50 dead attendants were then mounted on the horses' backs, kept erect by poles attached to their spines. This macabre mounted guard was then left to watch over the dead ruler, buried with him under a huge

earthen mound. No one has yet dug up a tomb exactly matching Herodotus's description, but they have found some that come close to it; in one mound in the Caucasus, for instance, the bodies of 29 horses were found interred in a circular trench, their heads all directed toward a central grave, presumed to be that of their owner.

The Pazyryk burials

More significantly, a series of burials unearthed more than 2,500 miles (4,000 km) away from the lands Herodotus visited have shown that there were extraordinary parallels

above: This fragment of a felt wall-hanging from a Pazyryk tomb, ca. 500–400BCE, depicts a nomadic clan warrior from the Scythian world, on horseback.

between the Scythians he described and the horse cultures of the steppelands where Siberia meets Mongolia and China.

The excavations took place in the Pazyryk region, an area of high grassland 5,250 feet (1,600 m) up in the Altai Mountains. The district is rich in burial mounds known as kurgans, some of which were cursorily excavated in the nineteenth century. The main work, however,

chambers, in which either one or two bodies were laid to rest in coffins made from hollowed logs. Both men and women were found interred in the mounds, which also contained the graves of horses, presumably sacrificed at the time of their owners' death. Some kurgans contained a single horse burial, but others housed as many as 14 equine skeletons.

The people who built the tombs were mounted sheep- and cattle-herders who had much in common not just with Herodotus's Scythians but also with Central Asian pastoralists to this day. Theirs was a warlike society, marked by constant conflicts over grazing land and by raids to seize cattle and booty. The mounds bore graphic testimony to the dangers involved. The occupant of one that Rudenko excavated had been bludgeoned to death with a battle-axe, while a body unearthed by Polosmak in 1995 bore the marks of a fatal wound to the stomach. Presumably both men had been warrior chieftains who died leading their warbands into battle.

Frozen in time

The Pazyryk corpses were preserved by ice, and had to be cut out of their tombs in frozen blocks. Most of the soil in the region is trapped in permafrost, but the top few feet unthaw enough each summer to allow for the digging of graves. Once the bodies were in the earth, however, the burial chambers

above: A detailed battle scene decorates this gold comb, found in the Solokha royal kurgan in the Ukraine. Dated to 430–390BCE, the comb is thought to have been made by a Greek craftsman for a Scythian client.

was done by the Soviet archaeologist Sergei Rudenko, first in 1929 and then after the Second World War in 1947–1949, and, more recently, by Natalya Polosmak, who took up the challenge between 1990 and 1995.

The kurgans that Rudenko and Polosmak excavated dated back to the years between 500 and 300BCE – an Iron Age era coinciding with Herodotus's visit to the Scythians. Above ground, the structures took the form of low earth mounds, sometimes topped by cairns of stones. Beneath the surface, the mounds concealed rectangular shafts 13–16 feet (4–5 m) deep. At the bottom lay wooden burial were covered over with logs and stones and then with earthen mounds. These insulating layers effectively turned the chambers into deep-freeze refrigerators, in which not just the bodies themselves but also other organic materials such as wood, leather and textiles survived the passage of more than two millennia relatively intact.

Mummification techniques

The preservation of the bodies also owed something to the mummification techniques applied to them before burial. The brains were removed, not through the nostrils as in Egypt but via a hole trepanned in the back of the skull. Long incisions were made in the body and in the limbs, and the internal organs were removed, along with some sections of the larger muscles. The inner spaces were then packed with grass, horsehair or other padding to restore the corpse's natural shape; in one case, a cranium was found to have been filled with a mixture of soil, pine needles and larch cones. Some sort of preservative fluid – possibly brine – seems also to have been injected into the bodies, some of which show signs of puncture marks. Finally, the slits were sewn up again with a thread of horsehair or animal sinew. Mummification no doubt helped to keep fresh the bodies of those people who had died in winter, enabling them to be preserved until the summer months when burials

took place once the severe freeze had eased and graves could be dug.

Herodotus vindicated

The unique conditions of the kurgans in effect turned them into time capsules, and among the biggest surprises they contain is evidence that much of what Herodotus wrote 2,400 years ago was true. His descriptions of the significance of tattooing for the Scythians, of their military prowess, of the practice of mummification, and of the raising of burial mounds have all been borne out. Even more striking was the confirmation provided for his story of drugged mourners. Small bronze stands for burning hemp were found in almost all the graves, along with small felt tents; and in one of the graves, two vessels were even found with charred hemp seeds still in place on top of them.

The Siberian Ice Princess

Not all the tombs found in the Pazyryk region were those of warriors. In 1993, Polosmak unearthed the undisturbed grave of a woman buried alone, not alongside a partner as in the case of previous female finds. The woman had apparently died of natural causes, aged about 25. She was evidently a person of distinction, to judge from the quality of the goods buried with her – wooden salvers containing cuts of mutton and horsemeat, gilded metal ornaments, leather and textile items, a decorated hand mirror. These objects were clearly intended to be of use to the deceased in the afterlife. In addition, the skeletons of six horses had been interred close to her burial chamber. The dead woman bore elaborate tattoos on her shoulder, wrist and thumb. Depicting abstract patterns and intricate animal forms, these tattoos may designate her as a shaman, or perhaps they were a mark of aristocratic status. She wore an unusually tall headdress made of felt on a wooden underframe, the shape of which recalls Western notions of a witch's hat.

Herodotus had described some Scythian tribeswomen as Amazons who joined their menfolk in battle, claiming they were not allowed to marry until they had killed an enemy. This woman, however, seems to have passed away peacefully and she has entered the popular imagination as the "Siberian ice princess".

CHINA'S IMPERIAL TOMBS

Recently some of the world's most exciting archaeological discoveries have been made in China, where the Communist government has actively encouraged fieldwork in the decades since the turmoil of the Cultural Revolution. Like the ancient Egyptians, the Chinese saw the afterlife as a continuation of life as it had been on Earth. Rulers had elaborate tombs prepared, equipped with everything they thought necessary to maintain their standard of living beyond the grave. As a result, imperial burial sites provide fascinating snapshots of Chinese court life from early times.

above: The Shang were firm believers in the power of oracles. To foretell the future, diviners wrote questions on animal bones or tortoiseshells such as this one, which they heated over a naked flame, reading the likely outcome from the pattern of cracks that formed.

The secrets of the Shang

The earliest burials yet discovered hark back to the Shang dynasty, traditionally dated to the Bronze Age years from 1766 to 1027BCE. This was an era when chariot-borne warriors with expensive metal weapons lorded it over peasants armed only with utensils of stone and bone. Shang warlords dressed in silk and occupied spacious houses with gabled roofs, which they decorated with expensive metal artefacts. At their head was a king credited with semi-divine powers, revered as the "Son of Heaven".

In their religious beliefs, the Shang venerated the spirits of dead ancestors while also recognizing the power of a supreme deity, Shangdi, and a host of nature gods. Numerous oracular inscriptions have been preserved that describe the royal ancestors' hunger for animal and human sacrifice; the diviners often sought to determine what type and scale of sacrifice would be the most auspicious.

The story that reopened the once-closed book of Shang history began in 1899. In that year Lie Tieyun, a Beijing scholar studying ancient scripts, happened to notice faint inscriptions on pieces of tortoiseshell being ground up for use in traditional Chinese medicines. He traced the shells back to Henan province in north-central China, where dealers were selling them as "dragon bones". More than 1,000 of the tortoiseshell inscriptions were eventually deciphered and revealed to be ancient oracles of the Shang kings.

Even so, the dealers continued to protect their sources, and it was not until the late 1920s that scholars finally tracked down the oracles' point of origin to the village of Xiaotun, near the town of Anyang. Many more inscriptions were subsequently found there: eventually over 100,000 were recovered.

In time the fields around Anyang turned out to hold more than just oracle bones. In the mid-1930s, 10 large royal tombs were discovered. All took the form of deep shafts of compacted earth, with ramps leading down to a burial area at their base. All had been plundered of their grave goods in antiquity. What the thieves had left, however, were the bones of the sacrificial victims killed when the dead kings were laid to rest.

The killings were on a huge scale. In one case, the bodies of 24 women lined the ramp on one side of a burial pit, and 17 men on the other. At the bottom were the remains of eight dogs, four to each ramp, along with eight two-horse chariot teams, each with the bones of two armed charioteers between the horses. The excavators also found more animal sacrifices – mostly monkeys and deer – and 34 human skulls. A group of 17 mass graves located close to the burial site yielded 160 decapitated skeletons.

The Anyang area has continued to produce major finds into recent decades. In 1976, a Chinese team turned up the first undisturbed royal tomb: that of Fu Hao, the favourite wife of one of the longest-lived Shang kings and a distinguished general in her own right. Although Fu Hao's body had entirely decomposed, the remains of 16 human sacrificial victims were found, along with the skeletons of six dogs. So too was a treasure of grave goods comprising more than 440 bronze objects, 700 jades, 560 bone artefacts, and almost 7,000 cowrie shells,

below: This partially collapsed bronze chariot, complete with driver, was among the many lifelike models discovered in the remarkable tomb of Qin Shihuangdi, the First Emperor (see page 139).

which were used as a currency at the time. Archaeologists were awe-struck by the extravagance of the burial, the artefacts' beauty, and the quality of the craftsmanship, all of which, they were soon to discover, set a pattern for imperial burials for hundreds of years to come.

Over the past few years further tombs dating from the Shang period have been discovered in Jiangxi, Hunan and Sichuan provinces, mostly more than 500 miles (800 km) from Anyang. The many remarkable bronze artefacts excavated at these sites suggest that the Shang coexisted with other advanced, independent Chinese cultures flourishing beyond the dynasty's frontiers. These discoveries suggest that the neat dynastic pattern laid out in the early Chinese histories may have concealed a more complex reality in which rival states with different ruling lineages lived side by side. In ancient times as today, it seems, Chinese civilization was far from homogeneous.

The First Emperor's final resting place

The Zhou dynasty that succeeded the Shang was the longest-lasting in Chinese history, but in its later stages it lost control over much of the country. China dissolved into the anarchy of the Warring States period, and central control disappeared. The man who restored it was the first ruler of the Qin dynasty, Shihuangdi, who reunited the nation and took the title of First Emperor. He then launched a revolutionary programme of policies designed to cement his dominions together: among other steps, he enforced a single set of laws on the empire, standardized weights and measures, and established the use of the Qin script throughout China.

Shihuangdi was a decisive and effective ruler, but also a ruthless one. In the last years of his life, he became obsessed with the idea of beating the final enemy: death. According to later historians, he sent a fleet in search of

left: Qin Shihuangdi's Terracotta Army is fronted by a vanguard of 200 lightly armed bowmen. Behind them, in 11 corridors, armoured infantrymen are lined up four abreast behind four-horse battle-chariots. The two outermost aisles contain archers, facing out to protect the flanks.

"Through the white mist, tear-
  dampened, the old woodcutter came
And gathered up the hair from
  Tz'u-hsien's tomb.
Black, seven feet long, its sheen lit
  up the ground.
Around the hair were two golden pins."

(EXTRACT FROM "LAMENT ON AN OLD HAIRPIN", WRITTEN BY THE LOYALIST SOUTHERN SUNG POET HSIEH AO, FOLLOWING THE DESECRATION OF SIX SUNG IMPERIAL TOMBS IN 1278 ON THE ORDERS OF THE MONGOL CONQUERORS)

an imagined "Island of the Immortals" that, according to his diviners, lay somewhere over the eastern ocean. The 3,000-strong crew were never seen again, and legend has it that they settled in Japan.

While seeking to extend his earthly life, however, Shihuangdi took care to prepare for the afterlife as well. Throughout his reign, a vast army of conscript labour worked on his mausoleum, located east of the town of Xian in a district rich in imperial graves. They created nothing less than an underground city, with ramparts 7.5 miles (12 km) long.

Shihuangdi's mausoleum was reportedly twice raided by his enemies in antiquity, but then was left to moulder undisturbed into modern times. A first inkling of the riches it might contain came in 1974, when members of a farming commune who were digging a well came upon fragments of statues of horses and soldiers. Further investigation revealed a huge rectangular pit, 750 feet (230 m) long and 200 feet (60 m) wide, filled with life-size model soldiers. This was the famous Terracotta Army (see illustration, opposite), designed to guard the emperor in death; it was believed that the statues would be magically animated in the afterlife. The excavation is still incomplete, but so far almost 8,000 figures have been recovered.

Additional wonders have since come to light. Subsidiary pits housed the army's cavalry division and general staff, this last containing two spectacular bronze chariots, each drawn by a team of four terracotta horses. A menagerie of live animals was also buried with the emperor, presumably to provide him with a private zoo beyond the grave.

Then there were the human victims. Several hundred common graves have been found in the complex's outer reaches that are thought to belong to the labourers who worked on the tomb, killed to protect its secrets. Other victims were buried alive when the emperor's body was laid to rest. In all, 48 imperial concubines were reportedly sent to their deaths in this way. The recent discovery of 17 decapitated bodies may indicate the fate of some of the emperor's younger sons. Archaeologists have speculated that they were killed on the orders of Shihuangdi's heir, Hu Hai, to remove rival claimants to the throne.

The centrepiece of the complex is the emperor's own tomb, located under a burial mound that still rises almost 165 feet (50 m) above the surrounding plain.

Immortal Jade

The ancient Chinese believe that jade conferred immortality and had the power to prevent bodily decay and ward off evil spirits. Elaborate jade death suits, such as the one made for Princess Dou Wan (see illustration, below) in the second century BCE, were the ultimate expression of this belief. Discovered in 1968 in the tomb she shared with her husband Lui Sheng in Mount Ling, 100 miles (160 km) southwest of Beijing, Dou Wan's suit is composed of more than 2,100 jade plaques, sewn together with gold wire. In 1996 an even more magnificent jade shroud was found in the tomb of Liu Wu, third king of the state of Chu during the Western Han dynasty (206BCE–9CE), in Lion Mountain in eastern Jiangsu province. More than 4,000 wafer-thin jade plaques were sewn together with gold thread to create the shroud, which is decorated with flowers and buttons also fashioned out of gold.

Inside, workers reportedly built a miniature model of the emperor's domains, complete with quicksilver replicas of the Yangtze and Yellow rivers marvellously contrived to flow eternally into an imitation sea. There the emperor's body was eventually laid to rest amid magnificent grave goods in 210BCE, protected, so the chronicles claimed, by loaded crossbows rigged up with tripwires to shoot down unwary tomb robbers. No one knows how effective the defences were, or how many of the tomb's contents still remain, for the mound itself has yet to be excavated; archaeologists are holding off until they are sure that they have the necessary preservation techniques to protect the treasures that may still lie inside.

Jing Di's tomb: statuettes and sacrificial victims

In 1990 workers building a road about 20 miles (30 km) west of the First Emperor's mausoleum came upon the remains of another imperial tomb complex. This one belonged to Jing Di, the fifth ruler of the Han dynasty, who ascended the throne in 157BCE. Excavations showed that he too had a terracotta retinue to accompany him in death, but a very different one from Shihuangdi's. The figures were only a third of the size of the Terracotta Army warriors, standing just 24 inches (60 cm) tall. When found, they were naked and armless, for their wooden limbs and silk raiments had long since rotted away. Also unlike Shihuangdi's attendants, they were not just military. Jing Di apparently preferred to be surrounded by his entire court in the afterlife, and so went to the grave surrounded by models of men, women and eunuchs along with horses, sheep, pigs and chickens.

Significantly, however, the twin tombs of Jing Di and his wife were surrounded by communal graves housing more than 10,000 bodies, scattered over more than a square mile (2.6 sq km). Most of the dead had been thrown into the earth without coffins, and many had been beheaded or cut in two. These grim discoveries seem to confirm historical records claiming that the mausoleum was built by an army of convict labourers, many of whom evidently either died on the job or were sacrificed when it was finished. Some were buried wearing the very same fetters that had kept them tied to the task when they were alive.

The sheer number of bodies found at the imperial burial grounds has startled scholars, who had previously assumed that the practice of human sacrifice tailed off at the end of the Bronze Age, almost 1,000 years before Jing Di's day. It now seems that the custom lingered, perhaps as a result of China's instinctive conservatism in ritual matters. It was even revived as late as the fourteenth century CE, when Zhu Yuanzhang, the first Ming emperor, gave orders for some of his own concubines to accompany him to the grave as part of a drive to restore old Chinese ways after the expulsion of the foreign Yuan dynasty. Imperial concubines continued to be killed and buried with their masters until the sixth Ming emperor finally banned the practice in the mid-fifteenth century.

Treasures awaiting discovery

Also located in Shaanxi province is the burial site of the Tang-dynasty monarch, Empress Wu. The mausoleum contains the bodies of the empress and her husband, the emperor Gaozong, who died in 683CE. Wu, who is said to have been a cruel and tyrannical ruler, outlived him by 22 years.

The Qianling site has a circumference of 25 miles (40 km) and contains 17 satellite tombs. Constructed to resemble a palace, the walled complex was approached along an imposing avenue known as a "spirit path" (see illustration, pages 124–5), lined with life-size statues of animals, officials and soldiers, who were perhaps intended to serve as a guard or else to form an everlasting funeral procession. More than 40 years after its discovery the imperial tomb itself, believed to contain a wealth of grave goods as well as the bodies of the two rulers, is still unopened.

As events of the last decade have shown, new finds are constantly forcing archaeologists to review their assumptions about China's imperial tombs and what they can tell us about the nation's history. We can only speculate as to what surprises still lie buried, waiting for excavators to reveal them.

KEYHOLE TOMBS OF JAPAN

Japan's most extraordinary prehistoric monuments take the form of vast tumuli, or tomb mounds. There are more than 10,000 of them in all – so many that they have given their name to an entire era of the nation's early history. The *kofun* ("ancient tomb") period (ca. 300–600CE) was a time when power was coalescing in the hands of a warrior aristocracy, grouped in clan-based states that competed fiercely for primacy. The mounds served to mark the graves of their chiefs.

The custom of singling out the burial places of powerful individuals had its roots in earlier times, when elite interments had taken place in dolmens. These sepulchres of massive stone, strikingly similar in appearance to their equivalents in western Europe, were often set apart from the communal cemeteries where the rest of the population was buried, surrounded by an isolating ditch or a grove of trees. The unhewn blocks that formed the burial chambers were originally covered over with earth, like their European counterparts, but over the course of the centuries the soil coating has often weathered away.

In the *kofun* era the mounds mushroomed beyond all recognition. Some continued to be circular in form, while others were square, rectangular or trapezoid in outline. The most distinctive ones, however, combined circle and trapezoid into a keyhole shape. And the biggest, such as Emperor Nintoku's mound (see illustration, below), were immense – more than 1,500 feet (480 m) long and over 100 feet (30 m) high.

The keyhole tombs share some general features. The burial chamber always lies in the circular end, where it is usually approached by a stone passageway entering from the side. The top of the circular mound is invariably the highest point; otherwise, the tomb's profile falls away to a low neck and then generally rises slightly to a platform at the far end of the squared-off section. In many cases the mounds are stepped in outline, with up to three shallow tiers, while the larger ones are protected from trespassers by one, two or even three separate, water-filled moats.

The tombs predate the earliest Japanese books, so there are no written records to explain why the keyhole shape came into use. The

left: Emperor Nintoku's mound, located in the town of Daisen near Sakai, is Japan's largest keyhole tomb. Built in 443CE, the mound is surrounded by a triple moat.

"Thereupon [Minister] Nomi no Sukune came forward and said, 'It is not good to bury living men upright in the tumulus of a prince. How can such a practice be handed down to posterity? I beg leave to propose an expedient that I will submit to your Majesty.' So he sent messengers to summon 100 clay workers from the land of Idzumo, and directed them to take clay and form the shapes of men, horses and various objects, which he presented to the Emperor, saying, 'Henceforth let it be the law to substitute things of clay for living men, and to set them up at tumuli'. Then the Emperor was well satisfied, saying, 'Your idea has greatly pleased our heart'."

(FROM THE *NIHONGI* [*CHRONICLES OF JAPAN*], CA. 720CE)

most likely explanation is that the square-ended section served as a temporary shelter for the body while the larger circular mound, with its more permanent stone burial chamber, was being constructed nearby. The two were then joined after the corpse had been transferred to its final resting-place.

The contents of the tombs

Traditionally many of the tombs have been identified with early emperors, and they are still treated with a degree of reverence in Japan; many have not been excavated. Some of those that have been explored were found to have been looted in antiquity, but others have yielded impressive grave goods. Weapons and armour are especially in evidence, suggesting that the tombs' occupants were warriors. Decorated bronze mirrors are also common. The mirrors were probably associated with the Shinto sun goddess Amaterasu, the mythical progenitor of Japan's imperial line: not only does their circular form suggest the shape of the sun's disc, but they also recall one of Japan's best-known legends, which tells how Amaterasu once hid her life-giving light in a cave, from which she was only

right: *Haniwa* dolls such as this warrior representation served as guardian-attendants to the departed during the *kofun* period.

tempted out by the sight of her own reflection in a mirror.

The damp earth of Japan discourages preservation, so no significant human remains have been found in the keyhole tombs. However, one intriguing clue to the lifestyle of the occupants is the presence of bridle bits, stirrups and saddle decorations among the mounds' contents. Horse-riding was a novelty in Japan at the time, leading some scholars to speculate that a new wave of mounted immigrants might have entered Japan from Korea or Manchuria, where a mound-building tradition already existed, bringing the *kofun* custom with them. Others, however, question the whole notion of largescale incursions, thinking it more likely that the native aristocracy adopted the equestrian habit themselves.

The early Japanese elite

The Japanese were certainly in touch with mainland Asia when the *kofun* period began, and had been for more than a hundred years. A Chinese document has survived containing reports from travellers to Japan in the mid-third century CE that provide intriguing glimpses of Japanese society in the decades immediately before the *kofun* era. It tells of an orderly agricultural world of peasant villages and marked

class distinctions. Men of rank had four or five wives; when ordinary citizens met them on the road, they were expected to squat or kneel with both hands on the ground as a gesture of respect.

The Chinese record also gives a tantalizing account of one of the rulers of early Japan – a priestess-queen identified as Himiko (the word means "princess") who "occupied herself with magic and sorcery … ". Himiko was said to live in a fortress-palace staffed by 1,000 women and

one man, who acted as her mouth-piece. On her death, the Chinese record claims, she was buried in an earthen mound more than 100 paces in diameter, accompanied in death by all her attendants.

Fascinating though it is, the Himiko story is unreliable: at best it is hearsay, retailed by a foreigner with little clear understanding of Japanese ways. In fact no archaeological evidence of human or animal sacrifice has yet turned up in Japan – unlike in China, where the practice was carried out on a grand scale in early times. Many scholars are sceptical of Himiko's very existence, and more doubt the reality of her burial, of which no physical trace has yet been found.

The sacrifice puzzle

Japanese sources too mention early traditions of sacrifice. They do so in the context of the earthenware objects called *haniwa* (literally, "rings of clay") that were among the *kofun* tombs' most distinctive features. Initially these shaped figurines were no more than their name suggests: simple tubular cylinders, sometimes as much as 5 feet (1.5 m) high, that were

left: Architectural *haniwa* were common too – this is probably a rice storehouse. The unglazed clay finish accentuates its *kami* or life-energy.

lined up in their hundreds around the tiers of the mounds, probably serving to hold the earth in place and stop slippages. Over time, however, they turned representational: there were *haniwa* in the form of animals, boats, buildings and everyday objects.

Above all, though, the *haniwa* took human form – and thereby hangs a tale. The *Nihongi* – Japan's earliest historical work, written in the eighth century CE – reports that an early emperor of Japan noted with sorrow the practice of human sacrifice when his younger brother died. One of his ministers then came up with an alternative for the next state funeral, which took place on the emperor's mother's death. He ordered clay models to be made to take the place of the deceased queen's living entourage (see quotation, page 143). From that time on *haniwa* replaced live victims – or so the story claimed.

Enshrined as it was in Japan's officially approved imperial archives, this account passed down virtually unchallenged for generations. Now, however, most scholars prefer to reserve judgment as to its accuracy. One day, perhaps, a previously unexcavated mound will provide evidence that court servants were buried alive with their masters – standing vertically in the posture of *haniwa* figures, if the *Nihongi* is to be believed. At present, though, the evidence tends to suggest that the story was an after-the-fact explanation of the origin of the models rather than a reflection of real events.

Japan's Royal Mummies

Mummification was never common in Japan, but for reasons that remain unclear four leaders of the Northern Fujiwara, one of the ruling clans of twelfth-century CE Japan, chose to have their bodies preserved in this way. The mummies have survived to the present day, housed in special containers in the Golden Hall of the Chuson-ji Temple in Hiraizumi. This extraordinary monument was built in 1124 by Kiyohira, the first of the four to be mummified, to serve as the family's private chapel, taking its name from the gold leaf that encased most of its exterior.

The Fujiwara mummies are all related: they are grandfather, father, son and grandson. The family to which they belonged had in effect ruled Japan for much of the Heian period (794–1185CE), but their branch had chosen to move from the capital to a northern region. There they became the dominant power at a time when centralized authority was collapsing and the nation was falling into the hands of local warlords. For most of the twelfth century they ruled northern Honshu as a semi-independent realm, offering only nominal fealty to the emperor in Heian (modern Kyoto).

The four chiefs who had themselves mummified were the last of the line – so much so that only the decapitated head of the last, Yasuhira, survives; he was beheaded after the fall of Hiraizumi, his capital, to hostile forces in 1189. The first of the quartet, Kiyohira, had died 61 years earlier at the age of 73; his son Motohira was mummified in 1157, and his grandson Hidehira (Yasuhira's father) in 1187, aged 66.

In 1950, a multidisciplinary team of scientists exhumed the bodies and subjected them to detailed examination. One goal was to find out whether they had mummified naturally or had been subjected to some form of embalming. Following detailed forensic investigation, the team decided that they had most likely been embalmed, although the damaged condition of the corpses made it hard to be sure; over the centuries, most of the internal organs had been eaten by rats.

ENIGMATIC EASTER ISLAND

Easter Island – so called because the first Europeans to visit it arrived on Easter Day – is one of the most remote inhabited spots on Earth. A triangle of volcanic rock in the eastern Pacific, it covers just 45 square miles (117 square km). Its nearest neighbour, Pitcairn Island, is 1,400 miles (2,250 km) away, while in the opposite direction the coast of Chile lies 2,300 miles (3,700 km) off.

The islanders' isolation only makes their artistic achievements the more astonishing. For Easter Island is littered with the remains of more than 700 huge stone statues averaging 13 feet (4 m) in height and 8–10 tons in weight. The island's mysteries have long puzzled scholars. Where did the people who erected these enormous figures come from? Why did they build them?

Recently, archaeological research on the island – including studies of the bodies of some of its long-dead inhabitants – has begun to reveal its secrets, but the new research has also raised yet more questions. How, for example, did a people decimated by starvation and civil war in the 1600s recover enough for Dutch explorers to report finding a healthy, thriving population in 1722?

The first Easter Islanders
Today Easter Island supports a population of about 1,900, nearly half of whom are immigrants from Chile. In the past, however, before the arrival of diseases brought by the Europeans, and raids by slave traders, it had a much denser population.

In 1994 the analysis of DNA samples taken from the skeletons of 12 late-prehistoric Easter Islanders finally proved what experts had long suspected – the island was first peopled by Polynesians. The immigrants probably arrived in the third or fourth century CE, as part of the great ocean-borne expansion that populated the eastern Pacific islands in the first centuries before and after the start of the Common Era. At some unknown point thereafter, to judge from the presence of non-native plants on Easter Island, contact must have been made with South America. The Norwegian anthropologist and adventurer Thor Heyerdahl argued that Inca sailors had made the voyage, staging the Kon Tiki raft expedition to make his point. Today, however, most scholars tend to think the traffic went the other way, pointing to the Polynesians' proven mastery of ocean travel to support their view. Whatever movement there might have been seems to have been very limited; the Easter Islanders were mostly left to their own devices.

The monument builders
The quarry where all the island's larger statues were cut lies on the slopes of a volcanic cone called Rano Raraku. Made of densely compacted small stones known as lapilli, the underlying volcanic tuff is easily worked with stone implements, providing an ideal raw material for sculpting. Unfinished statues show that the monumental figures were shaped and polished in situ in the quarry, still attached to the bedrock by a keel of tuff. They were only cut free as they neared completion.

The big figures seem to have been produced between 1000 and 1600 CE. They were designed to be displayed on ceremonial platforms known as *ahu*s. At one time there were as many as 260 *ahu*s scattered across the island. They came in various shapes, the most common being an extended platform up to 330 feet (100 m) from end to end. The statues were always placed facing inland, and were apparently a focus for worship.

There has been much discussion as to how people equipped only with Stone Age technology could have moved and raised such huge objects. Experiments in recent years have suggested that, given enough muscle power, the statues could have been moved over a series of stone rungs set into the ground at intervals of 3 feet (1 m) or so, particularly if they were carried on a wooden A-frame sledge. The A-frames could then have doubled as gantries to lift the statues into place on the *ahu*. Probably they were pulled up a wooden ramp

onto the platform and then shifted inch by inch toward the vertical against a rising cairn of stones.

Whatever the exact method used to erect the stone figures, the amount of labour involved must have been huge. One of the mysteries of Easter Island is why such a small community should have put itself to so much trouble. Implicit in that conundrum

is the problem of what the sculptures represented in the minds of those who put them up.

Answers to these questions are not easy to find, as the culture that produced the sculptures was dead by the time that researchers first arrived to investigate it. Although the islanders had their own unique script, called *rongorongo*, it too had fallen into

above: Easter Island has long been an enigma because of the huge statues that lie toppled across the terrain and the mystery that surrounds the disappearance of the civilization that created them.

disuse and remains largely undeciphered. Oral traditions have survived, however, to cast some light on the statues' enigmatic presence.

The statues were raised partly because the islanders had time on their hands. Easter Island's climate is temperate and equable, with temperatures hovering between 21°C and 25°C throughout the year. Providing food, through fishing, hunting birds, and the cultivation of sweet potato and other staples, could hardly have been a full-time occupation, and recreational opportunities were very limited.

Furthermore, the islanders had a tradition of communal labour, honed in the making and moving of the huge outrigger canoes that had carried them across the Pacific. The evidence of petroglyphs found on the island suggests the people also had stone-carving skills from an early time. The malleability of the island's tuff thus provided the final link in a chain of technological logic leading the Easter Islanders toward monumental statuary.

Mana and ancestor worship

The meaning of the sculptures for those who erected them is less evident. To judge from oral tradition, two concepts were important: ancestor worship and the Polynesian notion of *mana*. This last is a spiritual power that can reside in people or places, in ceremonial objects or certain special features of the landscape. All the indications are that the statues had *mana* aplenty. As for their significance, this seems to

below: An Easter Island petroglyph represents the "birdman" (left) – the title given to the man who swam out to the offshore nesting sea birds to obtain and bring back safely the first eggs each spring.

have been linked to the veneration of honoured elders. Perhaps these were clan founders or leaders, for the island's population, though small, was bitterly divided between extended-family groupings. Different *ahu*s may well have been the focus of rival tribal loyalties.

The descent into chaos

A lingering uncertainty hangs over the long-nosed stone faces. It concerns the fate of the people who produced them. After five or six centuries of uninterrupted production, they suddenly stopped making them and, from the evidence of the displaced statues scattered around the island, turned actively to destroying them instead.

The indications are that some upheaval struck the island, probably in the century before the arrival of the first European explorer, Dutchman Jacob Roggeveen, in 1722. Island tradition spoke of a civil war between rival groups known as the "long ears" and the "short ears". The long ears were a dominant caste who forced the short ears to labour on the statues' construction. Eventually the short ears rebelled and rejected the long ears' overlordship, tearing down the monuments that were the symbols of their subjection.

Whatever the truth of the legends, modern investigators have suggested that environmental degradation caused by the people themselves also played a part in the rising tensions. The island's ecology was always

"As among the ancient Maoris, those who had taken part in the meal were entitled to show their teeth to the relatives of the victim and say, 'Your flesh has stuck between my teeth'. Such remarks were capable of rousing those to whom they were addressed to a murderous rage … "

(ON THE ORAL TRADITION THAT CANNIBALISM EXISTED AMONG THE ISLANDERS; AN EXTRACT FROM *EASTER ISLAND – A STONE-AGE CIVILIZATION OF THE PACIFIC* BY ALFRED METRAUX, 1957)

fragile. There were (and are) no rivers or streams – until modern times, all water for cultivation had to be fetched from lakes in the craters of the three volcanoes. For similar reasons, only a small amount of the island's total area is suitable for agriculture; elsewhere, there is simply the bare rock of dried-up lava flows.

Most importantly, by the time Europeans arrived the island was virtually treeless. It now appears that the islanders, who probably used wood principally to move their giant statues around, eventually chopped down all the island's trees. Without wood, not only did the production of statues come to an end, but there was no material with which to build canoes for fishing; increased soil erosion damaged farming, and the island's bird-life, once an important source of food, died out.

Archaeologists have found small, carved figures dating from this period that portray emaciated individuals;

the islanders were starving, and it was not long before they began to turn on each other for control of the few resources that were left. The discovery of gnawed human bones in rubbish pits dating from the fifteenth century CE has recently proved what today's Easter Islanders have long believed: in that terrible period of scarcity and internal struggle some of their ancestors even practised cannibalism.

A contemporary petroglyph depicting a "birdman" figure (see illustration, opposite) may hold the key to the islanders' mysterious, albeit temporary, recovery. According to historical accounts, once a year representatives of each tribal group swam the mile (1.6 km) out to an offshore island to collect birds' eggs and race back with their bounty. The winning tribe was given privileged access to food for the next year. Thus a "fair" system of food distribution replaced conflict, and the island's population avoided destroying itself completely.

FURTHER READING

Magazine and Journal Articles

Alva, Walter. "Discovering the New World's Richest Unlooted Tomb" in *National Geographic*, Vol.174, No.4, October 1988.

Arriaza, Bernardo. "Chile's Chinchorro Mummies" in *National Geographic*, Vol.187, No.3, March 1995.

Connolly, R.C. "Lindow Man: Britain's Prehistoric Bog Body" in *Anthropology Today*, Vol.1, Issue 5, October 1985.

Hart Hansen, Jens P., Meldgaard, Jørgen and Nordqvist, Jørgen. "The Mummies of Qilakitsoq" in *National Geographic*, Vol.167, No.2, February 1985.

Ingham, John M. "Human Sacrifice at Tenochtitlán" in *Comparative Studies in Society and History*, Vol.26, Issue 3, July 1984.

Kenyon, Kathleen M. "Excavations at Jericho" in *Journal of the Royal Anthropological Institute*, Vol.84, Issue 1/2, January–December 1954.

Lancaster, C.S. and Pohorilenko, A. "Ingombe Ilede and the Zimbabwe Culture" in *The International Journal of African Historical Studies*, Vol.10, Issue 1, 1977.

Lawal, Babatunde. "Dating Problems at Igbo-Ukwu" in *The Journal of African History*, Vol.14, Issue 1, 1973.

Phillipson, D.W. & Fagan, Brian M. "The Date of the Ingombe Ilede Burials" in *The Journal of African History*, Vol.10, Issue 2, 1969.

Polosmak, Natalya. "Pastures of Heaven" in *National Geographic*, Vol.186, No.4, October 1994.

Sugiyama, Saburo. "Burials Dedicated to the Old Temple of Quetzalcoatl at Teotihuacan, Mexico" in *American Antiquity*, Vol.54, Issue 1, 1989.

Reinhard, Johan. "Peru's Ice Maidens" in *National Geographic*, Vol.189, No.6, June 1996.

Reinhard, Johan. "Sharp Eyes of Science Probe the Mummies of Peru" in *National Geographic*, Vol.191, No.1, January 1997.

Traill, David A. "Schliemann's Discovery of 'Priam's Treasure': A Re-examination of the Evidence" in *The Journal of Hellenic Studies*, Vol.104, 1984.

Books

Alva, Walter and Donnan, Christopher. *The Royal Tombs of Sipán*. University of California Press: Los Angeles, 1993.

Andrews, Carol. *Egyptian Mummies*. British Museum Publications: London, 1984.

Bahn, Paul G. (ed.) *Tombs, Graves & Mummies*. Phoenix: London, 1998.

Barber, Elizabeth Wayland. *The Mummies of Ürümchi*. Pan: London, 2000.

Bernal, Ignacio. *A History of Mexican Archaeology*. Thames and Hudson: London, 1980.

Bibby, Geoffrey. *Looking for Dilmun*. Collins: London, 1970.

Boyd, Robert and Silk, Joan B. *How Humans Evolved*. W.W.Norton & Co.: New York, 1997.

Brier, Bob. *Egyptian Mummies*. Michael O'Mara Books: London, 1996.

Brier, Bob. *The Encyclopedia of Mummies*. Checkmark Books: New York, 1998.

British Museum. *Frozen Tombs*. British Museum Publications: London, 1978.

Burl, Aubrey. *Circles of Stone: The Prehistoric Rings of Britain and Ireland*. Harvill Press: London, 1999.

Carver, Martin. *Sutton Hoo: Burial Ground of Kings?* British Museum Press: London, 1998.

Ceram, C.W. *Gods, Graves and Scholars*. Book Club Associates: London, 1978.

Chamberlain, Andrew T. and Pearson, Michael Parker. *Earthly Remains: The History and Science of Preserved Human Bodies*. British Museum Press, London: 2001.

Chippindale, Christopher. *Stonehenge Compete*. Thames and Hudson: London, 1983.

Cockburn, Aidan and Eve. *Mummies, Disease and Ancient Cultures*. Cambridge University Press: Cambridge, 1980.

Cotterell, Arthur. *The First Emperor of China*. Macmillan: London, 1981.

Cottrell, Leonard. *The Bull of Minos*. Pan Books: London, revised ed. 1955.

David, Rosalie. *Mummies: Unwrapping the Past.* Weidenfeld & Nicolson: London, 1997.

David, Rosalie and Archbold, Rick. *Conversations with Mummies.* HarperCollins/Madison Press: London, 2000.

de Camp, L. Sprague and Catherine C. *Citadels of Mystery.* Fontana/Collins: London, 1972.

Dunand, Francoise and Lichtenberg, Roger. *Mummies: A Journey through Eternity.* Thames and Hudson: London, 1994.

Editors of Time-Life Books. *Lost Civilizations.* Time-Life Books: Alexandria, Va., 1992–95. The following titles of this 20-volume series are of particular relevance:
– *Africa's Glorious Legacy*
– *Anatolia: Cauldron of Cultures*
– *The Celts: Europe's People of Iron*
– *China's Buried Kingdoms*
– *Early Europe: Mysteries in Stone*
– *Egypt: Land of the Pharaohs*
– *Etruscans: Italy's Lovers of Life*
– *Mesopotamia: The Mighty Kings*
– *Pompeii: The Vanished City*
– *Sumer: Cities of Eden*
– *Vikings: Raiders from the North*

el Mahdy, Christine. *Mummies, Myth and Magic in Ancient Egypt.* Thames and Hudson: London, 1989.

Fagan, Brian M. (ed.) *The 70 Great Mysteries of the Ancient World.* Thames and Hudson: London, 2001.

Fitton, J. Lesley. *The Discovery of the Greek Bronze Age.* Harvard University Press: Cambridge, Mass, 1996.

Flood, Josephine. *Archaeology of the Dreamtime.* Collins: Sydney, 1983.

Fowler, Brenda. *Iceman.* Pan: London, 2002.

Glob, P.V. *The Bog People.* Faber and Faber: London, 1969.

Glob, P.V. *The Mound People.* Faber and Faber: London, 1974.

Hansen, Hart., Jens, Peder., Meldgaard, Jørgen and Nordqvist, Jørgen. *The Greenland Mummies.* British Museum Press: London, 1991.

Harris, James E. and Weeks, Kent R. *X-Raying the Pharaohs.* Macdonald: London, 1973.

Hughes, Dennis D. *Human Sacrifice in Ancient Greece.* Routledge: London and New York, 1991.

Johanson, Donald C. and Edey, Maitland A. *Lucy: The Beginnings of Humankind.* Granada: London, Toronto, Sydney, New York, 1981.

Kenyon, Kathleen. *Digging Up Jericho: The Results of the Jericho Excavations 1952–1956.* Frederic A. Praeger Inc.: New York, 1957.

Leca, Ange-Pierre. *The Cult of the Immortal: Mummies and the Ancient Way of Death.* Paladin: London, 1982.

Leick, Gwendolyn. *Mesopotamia: The Invention of the City.* Penguin Books: London, 2001.

Littleton, C. Scott. (ed.) *Mythology.* Duncan Baird Publishers: London, 2002.

Mercer, John. *The Canary Islanders: Their Prehistory, Conquest, and Survival.* Rex Collings: London, 1980.

Molyneaux, Brian and Vitebsky, Piers. *Sacred Earth, Sacred Stones.* Duncan Baird Publishers: London, 2001.

Pearson, Michael Parker. *The Archaeology of Death and Burial.* Sutton Publishing: Stroud, Gloucestershire, 1999.

Prag, John and Neave, Richard. *Making Faces: Using Forensic and Archaeological Evidence.* British Museum Press: London, 1997.

Reid, Howard. *In Search of the Immortals.* Headline: London, 1999.

Rudenko, Sergei. (trans. M.W. Thompson.) *Frozen Tombs of Siberia: The Pazyryk Burials of Iron-Age Horsemen.* University of California Press: Los Angeles, 1970.

Schele, L. and Freidel, D. *A Forest of Kings.* W. Morrow & Co: New York, 1990.

Spindler, K. (trans. Ewald Osers.) *The Man in the Ice.* Weidenfeld & Nicolson: London, 1994.

Stringer, Christopher and Gamble, Clive. *In Search of the Neanderthals.* Thames and Hudson: London and New York, 1993.

Turner, R.C. and Scaife, R.G. (eds.) *Bog Bodies: New Discoveries and New Perspectives.* British Museum Press: London, 1995.

Wood, Michael. *In Search of the Trojan War.* Facts on File: New York, 1985.

Woolley, Leonard. *Ur of the Chaldees.* Herbert Press: London, 1982.

INDEX

Page numbers in *italics* refer to illustrations and captions.

A

Abd el-Rassuls 19–20

Abydos (Egypt), ship burials 96–7

Afanasevans 131

Africa 8–35

early man 10–13

emigration from 127

see also individual countries/cultures

afterlife belief(s)

Egypt 15–17

Etruria 87–8

Mayan 59

Agamemnon 118

agriculture, megalithic tombs and 76

Ahmose 20

ahus, Easter Island 146–7

Aigai (Greece) 120

akh 14

Akhenaten (Amenophis IV) 22, *23,* 26

Akhetaten (Armarna) 22

Akkadian (language) and Akkad 107

Alexander the Great 121, 122

Alpine Iceman, the 72–5, *73*

autopsy of 72–3

cause of death of 74–5

clothing/possessions of 73–4, *74*

DNA testing of 72, 75

identification of 72

radiocarbon dating of 72

X-ray examination of 74

Altai mountains 133

Alva, Walter 52–6

Amateratsu 144

Amenophis IV (Akhenaten) 22, *23,* 26

America 38–67

first humans in 38–9

first immigration 38

see also individual countries/cultures

Amesbury Archer (Stonehenge) 79

Ampato, Mount 64

Anatolia 122–3

ancestor worship

on Easter Island 148–9

Jericho skulls and 105

Andronicus, Manolis 120

Anemospilia (Cave of the Winds) (Crete) 114

animal sacrifice(s)

in China 140

Inca culture and 66, 67

Moche culture and 54

Pazyryk Nomads and 134

Scythians and 133

under Shang dynasty 137

ship burials and 96, 98

in Ur 110–11

ankh 15

Ankhesenamen 27

Antioch I 122–3

Anyang (China) 136–9

apes, evolution of 11

Ardipithecus 13

Armarna (Akhetaten) 22

Arriaza, Bernardo 42

Asia 126–49

early man in 126–7

Homo erectus in 126

Homo sapiens in 127

immigration 127

see also individual countries/cultures

Assurbanipal (King of Nineveh) 107

Atacama desert (Chile) 40, *41*

aten (Egypt) 22, 24

Australopithecus afarensis 13

Australopithecus bosei 12–13

autopsies

of Alpine Iceman 72–3

of Tutankhamun 29

Avebury (UK) 76

Ay (pharaoh) 24

Ayrton, Edward 22

Aztecs 51

human sacrifices and 51

Toltecs, influence of 63

B

ba 14, 17

Bahrain 112–13

ballcourt, Chichén Itzá 62

Bandiagara cliffs (Mali) 31, *31*

Beaker Culture

grave goods in 79

round barrows in 78–9

Beauty of Loulan, the 129

Bede 97–8

beehive tombs, Mycenae 119

Bering Straits 38, 39

Bibby, Geoffrey 113

Blue Demons, Tomb of the (Etruria)
89
body casts, Pompeii *90,* 91–2
bogs/marshes 82–5
   bodies found in 83
   human sacrifice at 82, 83–5
   as offertory sites 84–5
   preservation properties of 82–3
   punishment and 83–5
The Book of the Dead (Egypt) 16
Briard, Jacques 78
brine, as preservation technique 135
Britain, bog people 82
Bronze Age
   bog people 82, 83
   China, imperial tombs 136
   Jutland 80–81
   ship burials 96
   Tarim Basin 128–9
   Troy 119
Brugsch, Emil 20
Brunet, Michel 10
burial custom(s)
   of *Homo sapiens sapiens* 71
   Japan, keyhole tombs 144
   of Neanderthal man 71
   of Pazyryk Nomads 133–4
   of Scythians 132–3
   ship burials 98–9
Burnarbashi (Turkey) 116

C

Caernarvon, Lord 26
Canary Islands 34–5
cannibalism
   on Easter Island 149
   Neanderthal man and 70

canopic jars 14–15
   Tutankhamun *27*
capacocha, Inca 66
Carchemish (Syria) 109
Carnac (France) 76
Carter, Howard *26,* 26–9
Cave of the Winds (Anemospilia)
   (Crete) 114
cenote, at Chichén Itzá 60–62
Central America *see* America
Chachapoya people, the 45–7, *46*
   grave goods of 46
   mummification techniques of 46–7
   textiles of 46
chacmool 51, *60*
Chad 10
Champollion, Jean-François 14
Charon 89
Charun 89
Chichén Itzá 60–63
   ballcourt at 62
   Kukulcán and 61
   Sacred Cenote at 60–62
   sacrificial items from 61–2, *62*
   Temple of Kukulcán at *61*
   Temple of Warriors at *61*
   Toltecs, influence of 61, 62–3
   tzompantli (wall of skulls) at 62, 63, *63*
China, imperial tombs of 136–41
   in Bronze age 136
   Shang dynasty and *see* Shang dynasty
   Zhou dynasty and 139–41
Chinchorro culture 7, 40–43
   grave goods of 40
   mummification techniques of 41–2, *43*
   natural mummification and 41
   self-adornment and 40–41
Chiribaya region (Peru) 47

Christianity, Sutton Hoo and 97
Chuson-ji Temple (Japan) 145
cinery urns 88
Citadel (Teotihuacán) 50
clothing
   of Alpine Iceman 73–4, *74*
   of Qilakitsoq corpses 101
   of Tarim Basin corpses 129
"Clovis theory" 38–9
Cobo, Bernabé 66
computed topography (CT), Ampato
   mummy-bundle and 65
Corded Ware Culture 79
cremation, Macedon 120
Crete 114–15
cuneiform 106–107

D

Darwin, Charles 10
Davies, Theodore 24, 26
deforestation, Easter Island 149
Deir el-Bahri cache 18–21, *19*
   contents of 20
   recovery of 20–21
   robberies and 19–20
della Valle, Pietro 107
Denmark, bog people of 82
Dilmun 112–13
   grave goods from *112,* 113
divination, Shang dynasty and *136*
Djimdoumalbaye, Ahounta 10
DNA analysis
   of Alpine Iceman 72, 75
   of Easter Islanders 146
   of Kennewick Man 39
   of Tarim Basin corpses 129
Dogon culture 31

dolmen *see* megalithic tombs

Dou Wan (Chinese princess) 140

dromos 87

Dubois, Eugène 12, 126

E

early man

  in Africa 10–13

  Africa, emigration from 127

  in Asia 126–7

  on Easter Island 146

  in Europe 70–71

Easter Island 146–9

  *ahu*s on 146–7

  ancestor worship on 148–9

  cannibalism on 149

  deforestation of 149

  DNA analysis and 146

  early man on 146

  mana and 148–9

  oral traditions of 147–8

  rongorongo script of 147

  statues on 146–9

Ecclesiastical History of the English Nation (Bede) 97–8

Egtved girl, the 81

Egypt, ancient 14–29

  afterlife beliefs in 14–17

  Deir el-Bahri cache *see* Deir el-Bahri cache

  Middle Kingdom 16

  mummification in 14–15

  New Kingdom 14–15, 18

  Old Kingdom 14, 18

  royal cache *see* Deir el-Bahri cache

  ship burials in 96–7

  soul and, aspects of 14

Tomb 35 *see* KV 35

Tomb 55 *see* KV 55

tomb decoration in *15*, 15–16, *17*

tomb robberies in 18–20

Tutankhamun *see* Tutankhamun

Valley of the Kings 18

Elgin, Lord 118

El Kurru (Kush/Nubia) 30

Epic of Gilgamesh 107, 112

  Dilmun and 112

ethnicity, Tarim Basin corpses 128–9, 130–31

Etruria 86–9

  afterlife beliefs in 87–8

  grave goods in *86*, 88, *88*

  Greek influence on 86, 89

  prophecy in 89

  Rome and 89

  tomb decoration in *87*, 87–8

Europe 70–92

  Alpine Iceman *see* Alpine Iceman

  bog people *see* bogs/marshes

  early man in 70–71

  megalithic tombs in *see* megalithic tombs

  ship burials in *see* ship burials

  see also individual cultures/countries

evolution, theory of 10–11

F

Feathered Serpent, Teotihuacán 50

Fertile Crescent (Near East) 104

Flag Fen (UK) 84

Fletcher, Joann 25

Fu Hao (Chinese noblewoman) 137, 139

funeral rites *see* burial custom(s)

G

gallery graves 77

Gaozong (Chinese emperor) 141

Gavrinis tomb (France) *76–7*

Germania (Tacitus) 84

Germany, bog people of 82

Gilgamesh, Epic of 107, 112

Girsu (Sumeria) 107–108

Glob, Peter (*The Bog People: Iron Age Man Preserved*) 82

Goell, Theresa 123

Gokstad ship (Norway) 94, 96

  animal sacrifice and 96

  tomb robberies and 94

Gotland, ship burials in 96

Grauballe (Denmark) 82

grave goods

  of the Amesbury Archer 79

  of the Beaker Culture 79

  of the Chachapoya 46

  of the Chinchorro 40

  in Dilmun *112*, 113

  in Etruria *86*, 88, *88*

  of Fu Hao 137, 139

  Homo sapiens and 71

  of Igbo Ukwu 32

  of the Inca 65, 67

  in Japan *143*, 143–4, 144, *144*, 144–5

  of the Lord of Sipán 7

  in Macedon 120, *121*

  of the Moche culture 7, 54, *54*

  in Mycenae *118*, 119, *119*

  of Neanderthal man 71

  Oseberg ship and 95

  of Pacal 58, *58*, *59*

  of Qin Shihuangdi *137*, 139, *139*, 141

of the Scythians 133, *134*
of the Shang dynasty 137
ship burials and 95, 96
at Sutton Hoo *96*, 97, *99*
at Teotihuacán *49*, 50, *51*
of Tutankhamun 26–7, *28*, 28–9, *29*
in Ur 109, 110, *110*
Great Zimbabwe 32–3
Greeks, influence on Etruria 86, 89
Greenland 100–101
Grønvold, Hans 100
Guanche people, the (Canary Islands) 34–5
caves of *34*
Gundestrup Cauldron *84*, 85

H

Hall, H.R. 109
handicapped individuals, as bog people 83
haniwa (Japan) *143*, 144, *144*, 144–5
Hatshepsut (pharaoh), mortuary temple of 19, *19*
Heian period (Japan) 145
Herbert, Lady Evelyn 26
Herculaneum 90–93
Herodotus
and Egypt 14
and Mesopotamia 106
and Scythian burial rites 132–3, 135
Heyerdahl, Thor 146
Hidehira (Japanese nobility) 145
hierothesion (Nemrut Dag) 122–3
Himiko (Japanese queen) 144
Hiraizumi (Japan) 145

Hissarlik (Turkey) 116
Historia del Nuevo Mundo (Cobo) 66
Homo erectus 12
in Asia 126
Homo habilis 12
Homo neandethalensis see Neanderthal man
Homo sapiens
in Asia 127
burial customs of 71
in Europe 70–71
evolution of 11–12
grave goods of 71
Homo sapiens idaltu 127
Horemheb (pharaoh) 24
horse burials, Pazyryk Nomads 134
huacas (Inca) 66–7
Hughes, Dennis 115
human sacrifice
Aztecs and 51
bog people and 82, 83–5
Inca and 64–7, *66*
Japanese keyhole tombs and 144, 145
Jing Di and 141
Kerma and 31
Mayan 57
in Minoan civilization 114–15
in Moche culture 54, 55
Oseberg ship and 95
Qin Shihuangdi and 140
Scythians and 133
Shang dynasty and 137
ship burials and 95, 99
in Teotihuacán 50–51
Toltecs and 51, 62
in Ur 110–11
Human Sacrifice in Ancient Greece (Hughes) 115

Hunan province (China) 139
Huxley, T.H. 10–11

I

Ibn Fadlan 98–9
Ica valley (Peru) 47
Iceman, the *see* Alpine Iceman, the
ice preservation, Pazyryk Nomads 134–5
Igbo Ukwu bronzes (Nigeria) 32
Iliad, the 117–18
Inca, the
animal sacrifices and 66, 67
capacocha and 66
grave goods and *65*, 67
huacas and 66–7
human sacrifice and 64–7, *66*
mummification and 44–5
mummy-bundles and 64–7
nature worship and 67
sacred mountains of 66–7
Ingombe Ilede (Zambia) 33
Iron Age, bog people 82, 83

J

jade, in burial 58, *59*, 140, *140*
Japan
Heian period in 145
kofun period in 142, 144
mummification in 145
Japan, keyhole tombs of *142*, 142–5
burial customs and 144
grave goods in *143*, 143–4, *144*, 144–5
human sacrifice and 144, 145
structure of 142

Java Man 126

Jericho skulls *104*, 104–105

    ancestor cults and 105

Jerusalem, tombs 105

Jiangxi province (China) 139

Jing Di (Han-dynasty ruler) 141

Jutland 80–81

K

ka 14

Kennewick Man (USA) 39

Kenyanthropus platyops 13

Kenyon, Kathleen 104–105

Kidron valley (Jerusalem) 105

Kiya (Egyptian princess) 24, *24*

Kiyohira (Japanese nobleman) 145

Klippel-Feil syndrome, Tutankhamun

    and 29

Knossos (Crete) 114

kofun period (Japan) 142, 144

Koldewy, Robert 109

Korfmann, Manfred 116

Kukulcán, Chichén Itzá 61

El Kurru (Kush/Nubia) 30

Kush/Nubia 30–31

KV 35 (Egyptian tomb) 25

KV 55 (Egyptian tomb) 22–5

    contents of 24

    mummies found in 24–5

L

Lambayeque (Peru) 52–6

Landa, Diego de 60

Layard, Austen Henry 107

Leakey, Louis 12–13

Leakey, Mary *10*, 12–13

Lhuillier, Alberto Ruz 56–8

Lie Tieyun (Chinese scholar) 136

Lindow Man (UK) 85

Linear pottery people 76

Ling, Mount (China) 140

Lion gate, Mycenae 119

Liu Wu (Chinese king) 140

Locmariaquer (France) 76

long barrows 77

Longgupo Cave (China) 126

Looking for Dilmun (Bibby) 113

Lord of Sipán (Moche culture) *52–3*,

    52–6

    discovery of 52–3

    grave goods of 7

    see also Moche culture

Loulan, the Beauty of 129

"Lucy" 13

Lui Sheng (Chinese prince) 140

M

Macedon 120–21

    cremation in 120

    grave goods in 120, *121*

Mali 31–2

mana, Easter Island 148–9

Mansa Musa (Malian emperor) 31

Mauch, Karl 32–3

Maya, the 56, 60

    afterlife beliefs of 59

    human sacrifice and 57

    see also Palenque

megalithic tombs 76–9

    agriculture and 76

    social changes and 76

    structure of 76–8

    see also individual types

Meroë 30

Mesopotamia 106–11

    Herodotus and 106

Middle Kingdom (Egypt) 16

"Millennium Man" 13

Minoan civilization 114–15

"missing links" 11

Moche culture 52–6

    animal sacrifice in 54

    development of 52

    grave goods of 7, 54, *54*

    human sacrifice and 54, 55

    warrior-priests of 55

    see also Lord of Sipán

Monte Verde (Chile) 38–9

Moon, Pyramid of the (Teotihuacán)

    50

mortuary temple, Hatshepsut 19, *19*

Motohira (Japanese nobleman) 145

mountains *see* individual names

mummies/mummification

    brine and 135

    Chachapoya 46–7

    Chinchorro 41–2, *43*

    in Egypt 14–15, 24–5

    Guanche 34–35, *35*

    Inca 44–5

    in Japan 145

    Pazyryk nomads and 135

mummies/mummification, natural

    Chinchorro 41

    Qarqan man 129–30, *130*

mummy-bundles *44*, 44–7

    Inca 64–7

mummy-dust 16

Mycenae 118–19

    grave goods in *118*, 119, *119*

mystery cults, Pompeii *93*

N

nabid 98

Napata (Nubia/Kush) 30

natron 15

natural mummification *see* mummies/
   mummification, natural

nature worship, Inca 67

Neanderthal man 70–71

   burial customs of 71

   cannibalism and 70

   disappearance of 70

   evolution of 11–12

   grave goods of 71

Near East 104–23

   see also individual countries/cultures

Nefertiti (Egyptian queen) 22, *23*

   mummy of 25

Nemrut Dag (Turkey) 122–3, *123*

Nerthus 85

Netherlands, bog people 82

Newgrange tomb (Ireland) *78*

New Kingdom (Egypt) 14–15, 18

Niebuhr, Carsten 107

Nigeria 332

Nihongi (Japan) 145

Nikolyasen, Nikolas 94, 96

Nineveh 107

Nintoku (Japanese emperor) 142

Nok sculptures (Nigeria) 32

North America *see* America

Nubia *see* Kush/Nubia

Nuri (Kush/Nubia) 30

"Nutcracker Man" 12–13

O

offertory sites, bogs/marshes 84–5

Old Kingdom (Egypt) 14, 18

Olduvai Gorge (Africa) 12

Olmecs 49

Oppert, Jules 107

Ordoñez, Ramon 56

Orrorin tugenensis 13

Oseberg ship (Norway) 95

Osiris (Egyptian god) 15, 16

P

Pacal (Mayan king) 58–9

   grave goods of 58, *58, 59*

   see also Palenque

Pacific 126–49

Palenque (Mayan city) 56–9

   "Red Queen" of 59

   Temple of the Inscriptions at 56–7,
      57

   see also Maya, the; Pacal

panaca (Inca) 44

Paracas (Peru) 45–7

passage tombs 76–7, *76–7, 77, 78*

Pausanias (Greek historian) 118–19

Pazyryk Nomads 132–5

   animal sacrifice and 134

   burials of 133–4

   ice preservation and 134–5

   mummification techniques of 135

   tomb decoration and *133*

   see also Scythians, the

Pekin Man 12, 126–7

Peru 44–7

Philip II of Macedon *120,* 120–21

Philip III Arrhidaeus 121

Pichu Pichu (Peru) 64

Pinudjem II (pharaoh) 21

Place of Fright (Xibalba) 59

Pliny the Younger 90

Polosmak, Natalya 134, 135

Pompeii 90–93

   body casts from *90,* 91–2

   mystery cults in *93*

preservation properties, bogs/marshes
      82–3

Priam (Trojan king) 119

prophecy, Etruscans 89

Puabi, Queen (Ur) 110, 111

punishment, bogs/marshes 83–5

Puruchuco-Huaquerones (Peru) 45

Pyramid of the Moon (Teotihuacán) 50

Pyramid of the Sun (Teotihuacán)
      49–50

pyramids, Nubia 30

Q

Qarqan man 129–30, *130*

Qawrighul 131

Qianling (China) 141

Qilakitsoq corpses 100–101

Qin Shihuangdi (First Emperor of
      China) 139–41

   animal sacrifice and 140

   grave goods of *137,* 139, *139,* 141

   human sacrifice and 140

   tomb robbery and 139

Queen Nefertiti *see* Nefertiti
      (Egyptian queen)

Tiy (Egyptian queen) 24

Quetzalcoatl, Teotihuacán 50

Qurna (Egypt) 18–19

R

radiocarbon dating
   of Alpine Iceman 72

of Beauty of Loulan 129
of bog people 82
of Qilakitsoq corpses 100
Raedwald (East Anglian king) 97–8
Ramapithecus 11
Ramesses I 20
Ramesses II 20, *21*
Ramesses IV, sarcophagus *17*
Ramesses IX 18
Rano Raraku (Easter Island) 146
Rawlinson, Sir Henry 107, 108, 112
"Red Queen", Palenque 59
Reinhard, John 64
Reisner, George A. 30
Reliefs, Tomb of the (Etruria) *87, 88*
Roggeveen, Jacob 149
Rome, influence on Etruria 89
rongorongo script, Easter Island 147
round barrows 77
    Beaker Culture and 78–9
Royal Cache *see* Deir el-Bahri cache
Rudenko, Serge 134

S

saché 61
Sacred Cenote, Chichén Itzá 60–62
sacred mountains, Inca 66–7
Sahel region (Africa) 10
Sakellarakis, Yiannis and Evi
    114–15
Sara Sara (Peru) 64
Sargon of Akkad 107, 112
Sarzec, Ernst de 107
Scandinavia 7
    ship burials in 94
    see also individual countries/cultures
Schliemann, Heinrich 116–19

Scythians, the 132–3
    burial rites of 132–3, 135
    grave goods of 133, *134*
    mummy skull *132*
    see also Pazyryk Nomads
Seleucus 122
self-adornment, Chinchorro 40–41
Seti I, mummy 20
    examination of 21
shabti figures 15–16
    in Nubia 30
Shang dynasty (China) 136–9
    animal sacrifice and 137
    divination and *136*
    grave goods and 137
    human sacrifice and 137
Shaw, Thurstan 32
Shihuangdi *see* Qin Shihuangdi (First
    Emperor of China)
ship burials 94–9
    in Abydos (Egypt) 96–7
    animal sacrifice and 98
    in Bronze age 96
    burial rites and 98–9
    in Gotland 96
    grave goods and 95, 96
    human sacrifice and 95, 99
    in Scandinavia 94
    standing stones and 96
Shona people 32–3
Siberian Ice Princess 135
Sichuan province (China) 139
Silk Road 128, 131
Simon, Helmut 72
Sipán, Lord of *see* Lord of Sipán
    (Moche culture)
skulls, wall of (*tzompantli*), Chichén
    Itzá 62, 63, *63*

Smenkare (pharaoh) 22
    mummy of 24–5
South America *see* America
standing stones, ship burials and 96
statues, Easter Island 146–9
Stonehenge 76
Sumeria 106–11
    city of Girsu 107–108
Sun Chariot 80–81, 85
Sun, Pyramid of the (Teotihuacán)
    49–50
Sutton Hoo 97–8
    grave goods from *96, 97, 99*

T

Tacitus (Roman historian) 84
Taklamakan Desert *128,* 128–31
Tarim Basin, Bronze Age 128–9
Tarim Basin corpses 128–31
    clothing of 129
    DNA testing of 129
    ethnic origins of 128–9, 130–31
Taylor, J. E. 108
Tell al-Ubaid (Syria) 109
Tellem people, the 31
Telloh (Iraq) 107–108
Tello, Julio 46–7
Temple of Kukulcán (Chichén Itzá) *61*
Temple of Quetzalcoatl (Teotihuacán)
    50
Temple of the Inscriptions (Palenque)
    56–7, *57*
Temple of Warriors (Chichén Itzá) *61*
Tenochtitlán (Aztec) 51
Teotihuacán *48,* 48–50
    the Citadel 50
    grave goods in *49,* 50, *51*

human sacrifice in 50–51
  Pyramid of the Moon 50
  Pyramid of the Sun 49–50
  Quetzalcoatl (Feathered Serpent)
      and 50
Terracotta Army 139, *139*, 141
textiles, Chachapoya 46
Thompson, Edward H. 61, 63
Thurnam, John 77–8
Tiy (Egyptian queen) 24
Tlaloc 51
Tlatilco, Tomb of 50–51
Tocharian 131
Tollan (Toltec capital) 51, 62
Tollund Man (Denmark) 82, *83*
Toltecs 51
  Aztecs, influence on 63
  Chichén Itzá, influence on 61,
      62–3
  human sacrifice and 51, 62
Tomb 35 *see* KV 35 (Egyptian tomb)
Tomb 55 *see* KV 55 (Egyptian tomb)
tomb decoration
  in Egypt *15*, 15–16, *17*
  in Etruria *87*, 87–8
  Pazyryk Nomads and *133*
Tomb of the Blue Demon (Etruria) 89
Tomb of the Reliefs (Etruria) *87*, 88
Tomb of Tlatilco 50–51
tomb robberies
  Deir el-Bahri cache 19–20
  in Egypt 18–20
  Gokstad ship and 94
  Qin Shihuangdi and 139
  in Ur 111
"Toumai" 10, *11*
"Treasure of Priam" 119
Tres Ventanas cave (Peru) 47

Troy 116–19, *117*
  in Homer's *Iliad* 117–18
Trundholm (Denmark) 80
Trundholm Chariot 80–81, 85
Tuchulcha 89
Tutankhamun (pharaoh) 22
  examination of mummy of 29
  grave goods of 26–7, *27*, *28*, 28–9,
      29
  tomb of *26*, 26–9
Tuthmose I 20
Tuthmose II 20
Tuthmose III 20
tzompantli (wall of skulls), Chichén
      Itzá 62, 63, *63*

U
Uhle, Max 40
Ur 106–111, *108–109*
  grave goods in 109, 110, *110*
  sacrifice in 110–111
  tomb robberies in 111

V
Valley of the Kings 18
  KV 35 *see* KV 35 (Egyptian tomb)
  KV 55 *see* KV 55 (Egyptian tomb)
Vanth 89
Vega, Garcilaso de la 67
Volterra tombs (Etruria) 86–8

W
wall of skulls (*tzompantli*), Chichén
      Itzá 62, 63, *63*
warrior-priests, Moche culture 55

Wedgwood, Joseph 86
Weigall, Arthur 22
Weighing of the Heart (Egypt) 17
"The Woman of Ancón" 47
Woolley, Leonard 109–110
Wu (Chinese empress) 141

X
Xenophon, Mesopotamia 106
Xibalba (Place of Fright) 59
X-ray examination
  of Alpine Iceman 74
  of Tutankhamun 29

Y
Yasuhira (Japanese nobleman) 145

Z
Zárate, Miguel 64
Zhou dynasty (China) 139–41
Zhoukoudian caves (China) 126–7
Zhu Yuanzhang (Ming emperor) 141
ziggurats 108
Zimbabwe 32–3, *33*

PICTURE CREDITS

The publisher would like to thank the following people, museums and photographic libraries for permission to repoduce their material. Every care has been taken to trace copyright holders. However, if we have omitted anyone we apologise, and will, if informed, make corrections in any further edition.

1 AA/Archaeological Museum, Lima/Dagli Orti; 2 Keren Su/Corbis; 5 O. Louis Mazzatenta/National Geographic Image Collection; 6 Ted Spiegel/Corbis; 7 Kevin Schafer/ Corbis; 8–9 Torleif Svensson/Corbis; 10 John Reader/Science Photo Library; 11 Getty Images/AF; 12 Science Photo Library/George Roos & Peter Arnold; 15 AA/Dagli Orti; 16 Sandro Vannini/ Corbis; 17 Gianni Dagli Orti/Corbis; 19 Roger Wood/ Corbis; 21 AA/Jacqueline Hyde; 23 AA/Egyptian Museum, Cairo/Dagli Orti; 24 Peter Clayton; 26 Underwood & Underwood/Corbis; 27 AKG/Erich Lessing; 28 Roger Wood/Corbis; 29 WFA/Egyptian Museum, Cario; 30 WFA/Museum of Mankind; 31 WFA; 33 Corbis/MIT Collection; 34 Archivo Iconografico/SA/Corbis; 35 Archaeological Museum Tenerife; 36 Danny Lehman/Corbis; 38 South American Library/Sue Mann; 39 Montana Historical Society Gift of Faye Case in memory of Ben Hargis; 41 South American Library/Robert Francis; 43 Bernardo Azziaza; 44 AA/Archaeological Museum, Lima/Album/ J.Enrique Molina; 45 AA/ Archaeological Museum, Lima/Dagli Orti; 46 Corbis/Engel Bros. Media; 48 Gianni Dagli Orti/Corbis; 49 AA/National Anthropological Museum, Mexico/Dagli Orti; 51 AA/National Anthropolgical Museum, Mexico/ Dagli Orti; 52–53 Heinz Pleuge/ RHPL; 54 Gianni Dagli Orti/ Corbis; 57 South American Library/Tony Morrison; 58 Copyright Merle Greene Robertson, 1976;

59 AA/National Anthropological Museum, Mexico/Dagli Orti; 60–61 RHPL/Odyssey/ Chicago; 62 AA/Mireille Vautier; 63 RHPL; 65 Maria Stenzel/National Geographic Image Collection; 66 Charles and Josette Lenars/Corbis; 67 John Bigelow-Taylor; 68–69 Bob Krist/ Corbis; 71 AKG Images; 73 Paul Hanny/Gamma/Katz; 74 South Tyrol Museum of Archaeology, Italy; 76-77 AA/Dagli Orti; 78 AA/ Dagli Orti; 79 Trust of Wessex Archaeology; 80–81 Copenhagen National Museum/DBP; 83 SPL/Silkeborg Museum, Denmark/ Munoz-Yague; 84 AA/National Museum, Copenhagen, Denmark/Dagli Orti; 86 AA/ Archaeological Museum, Florence/Dagli Orti; 87 Corbis/ Archivo Incongrafico, SA; 88 Araldro de Luca/Corbis; 90 AA/Dagli Orti; 91 AA/ Dagli Orti; 93 AA/Villa of the Mysteries, Pompeii/Dagli Orti; 94 WFA/State History Museum, Stockholm; 95 WFA/ Viking Ship Museum, Bygdoy, Norway; 96 British Museum; 99 AA/ British Museum/ Eileen Tweedy; 101 WFA/The Greenland Museum; 102–103 Nik Wheeler/Corbis; 104 Ancient Art & Architecture; 105 Charles & Josette Lenars/Corbis; 106 AKG-Images/Erich Lessing; 108–109 David Lees/Corbis; 110 British Museum/ DBP; 111 Adam Woolfitt/ British Museum/RHPL; 112 Adam Woolfitt/Bahrein Manama Museum/RHPL; 113 RHPL; 114 Bridgeman/National Archaeological Museum, Athens, Greece; 117 AA/Dagli Orti; 118 Ancient Art & Architecture Collection; 119 Ancient Art & Architecture Collection; 120 AA/Chiaramonti Museum, Vatican/Dagli Orti; 121 AA/Archaeological Museum, Salonica/Dagli Orti; 123 Chris Hellier/Corbis; 124–125 Corbis/Lowell Georgia; 126 Massino Mastrorillo/ Corbis; 127 John Reader/Science Photo Library; 128 RHPL; 130 Jeffery Newbury/Corbis/ Sygma; 132 AA; 133 Novosti, London; 134 AA; 136 WFA; 137 Index/ Summerfield; 138 Index/Summerfield; 140 AKG, London/Erich Lessing; 142 George Gerster/Network Photographers; 143 Corbis/ Seattle Art Museum; 144 Corbis/Sakamoto Photo Research Laboratory; 146 RHPL/G. Renner; 148 James. L Amos/Corbis